D0374971

BEGINNING TEACHING IN THE SECONDARY SCHOOL

BEGINNING TEACHING IN THE SECONDARY SCHOOL

Joan Dean

OPEN UNIVERSITY PRESS
Buckingham · Philadelphia

Open University Press
Celtic Court
22 Ballmoor
Buckingham
MK18 1XW

and
1900 Frost Road, Suite 101
Bristol, PA 19007, USA

First Published 1996

A catalogue record of this book is available from the British Library

ISBN 0 335 19619 5 (pb) 0 335 19620 9 (hb)

Library of Congress Cataloging-in-Publication Data
Dean, Joan.
    Beginning teaching in the secondary school/Joan Dean.
        p.   cm.
    Includes bibliographical references (p.   ) and index.
    ISBN 0–335–19620–9 – ISBN 0–335–19619–5 (pbk.)
    1. High school teaching – Great Britain.   2. Classroom management –
Great Britain.   I. Title.
LB1737.G7D43   1996
373.11'02 – dc20   96–33767
                                                                          CIP

Typeset by Type Study, Scarborough
Printed in Great Britain by Biddles Ltd, Guildford and King's Lynn

CONTENTS

1

INTRODUCTION

Teaching in a secondary school is a very demanding occupation. It is also very rewarding when you are able to do it well, and has consequences for the future which you can only partly anticipate. Hamblin (1978: xv), in the preface to his book *The Teacher and Pastoral Care*, notes how teaching called for every scrap of integrity, intelligence and imagination that he possessed, but, he says, 'the sense of excitement still persists'. Young people taught by teachers in whom this sense of excitement still persists are fortunate.

Yet it is not enough to care about young people and be committed to the work and excited by it. You need skills and knowledge, and although you may come into the work with a body of knowledge and know something of the skills you need, it is only through practice that these become part of your personal style as a teacher and work successfully. This takes time. You also need to work to maintain your knowledge, both of your subject area and of the psychology and sociology of teaching.

Secondary schools have seen considerable changes in recent years. The enormous development of human knowledge has made societies generally much more critical of what is done in schools and the competition for trade has made industry demand much more of school leavers than was formerly the case. Unskilled jobs are disappearing and this means that we need a more skilled workforce. We can no longer afford to concentrate our attention in schools on those able to achieve academically and be content to give others a good social education. We need to educate all young people to a higher level than in the past.

The development of technology of all kinds is also changing society. The advent of the computer has made knowledge much more widely available, and schools are gradually developing ways of enabling their students to benefit from this development.

As a result of these changes education has become a more political issue. It has become more costly and this alone makes it a political matter. In the past decade successive governments have passed a number of laws about education and have laid down much that schools must do, including the National Curriculum. This has had both good and bad results. Schools and teachers are under more pressure than they were formerly, but the evidence from Ofsted (Office for Standards in Education) and from examination results would seem to be that the National Curriculum is raising standards to some extent. Local management of schools (LMS) has made it possible for schools to make decisions about many issues which were formerly the province of the LEA (local education authority), and most schools feel that this has been a benefit, although most would also complain that the money is inadequate.

SOME AIMS

Schools are now required to have a statement of general aims, and within most departments in secondary schools aims have also been stated. Teachers need not only to bear in mind the school aims and the departmental aims but also to complement these with personal aims for both the students and themselves. There are a number of general aims for education in today's world that teachers need to bear in mind.

Young people need to become independent learners. The expansion of knowledge and the changes in the working environment mean that young people need to know more and be more skilled than formerly. They also need to be good learners because they will have to learn afresh on many occasions in their working lives. The ability to learn independently is now very important, and we should be aiming at a situation where all school leavers are able to learn without a teacher, a goal which we are at present very far from achieving, even with able students. All teachers should be concerned with the study skills relevant for studying their particular subject and study skills more generally.

Students need to develop skill in working with others. Much work today requires people to work in groups, each person contributing to group goals. Schooling in the past has been an individual process. This is changing with the demands of the National Curriculum, which requires work in groups, and schools need to take this aspect of learning seriously. We still have a lot to learn about how to do this and in particular how to assess work done in a group situation. Developing the ability of students to work cooperatively in groups should be an aim for all teachers.

Young people need the confidence and flexibility to cope with change. We do not know what the world will be like when our present secondary school students are adult. It seems likely that they will experience many changes during their adult lives and will need to be confident, flexible, able to cope with change, inventive, able to take initiative and able to learn afresh as new demands are made. We need to help them to develop these abilities.

Much learning needs to be seen to be applicable to real-life situations. Learning in school is intended as a preparation for life. This means that teachers need to think hard about the uses of what they are teaching and make these clear to students. The more that students can apply what they are learning in real-life situations the more they will be motivated to learn. Teachers need to look for opportunities for students to apply what they are learning to life outside school. On the other hand, there will also be learning in school that may not seem to have immediate relevance to life outside school, but will be part of the process of developing well-educated adults who will be able to look back on what they learned in school and see its relevance at a much later stage in their lives.

Young people need preparation for citizenship, including employment. Today's young people are growing up in a world where what happens in one part of the globe affects what is happening in other parts to a degree that is unprecedented. As adults they will be world citizens and need understanding of and sympathy with other people, including those whose lives are very different from their own. They will need to be tolerant of differences and learn to avoid stereotyping. They will also need knowledge of how our democracy works and their responsibilities and rights as citizens of this country. They are also growing up as citizens of Europe and need the skills to work in other countries. The ability to speak other languages is becoming increasingly important. Preparation for employment is important, including not only skills and knowledge but also qualities like integrity, honesty, reliability, punctuality, loyalty and readiness to work hard and give good value.

We need to prepare young people for leisure. The gradual automation of industry means that many people will have leisure forced upon them. It may be that we shall eventually recognize that everyone needs to work shorter hours so that there are more jobs, or more jobs will materialize in service industries which employ more people. Others will find themselves unemployed for periods. This suggests that we still need to take seriously preparation for leisure. Young people need to develop interests and hobbies which encourage them to use their spare time profitably and to enjoy leisure. Every subject has something to offer here and the attitude towards the subject developed by individual students will determine whether they see it as an area in which it would be interesting to go on learning and exploring. In particular students need to develop confidence in their ability to learn and to manage their own lives and a positive self-image.

These are the general aims, which go along with more specific aims about learning in the various aspects of the National Curriculum.

All teachers need to be concerned with the way students think and feel. Students' feelings about what they are learning affect their interest and ability to learn. Their feelings about other people, both teachers and students, affect their ability to relate to them. Students learn best from teachers they like and respect.

Hargreaves (1984: 2) suggested that there are four distinct aspects of learning with which a secondary school should be concerned. These are:

- written expression, the capacity to retain propositional knowledge and select from it in order to answer questions;
- the capacity to interpret and apply knowledge;
- personal and social skills;
- motivation and commitment, the willingness to accept failure without destructive consequences, readiness to persevere and the self-confidence to learn in spite of the difficulty of the task.

THE CONTEXT OF EDUCATION

We are currently experiencing a major change in the way teachers are trained, in that some teachers are now becoming qualified through a school-based training scheme. This places a new responsibility on the schools taking part in the scheme, and it remains to be seen whether this will result in more effective training. It will still be important for student-teachers to acquire knowledge of theories of teaching and learning, and this is likely to involve higher education. It should be possible for the theory to become much more closely related to work in the classroom.

The advent of GCSE (General Certificate of Secondary Education) changed the way many teachers worked and provided opportunities for a much wider range of students to achieve success in examinations. The National Curriculum has also changed the way teachers work, although this has varied somewhat from one subject to another and changes have posed considerable problems in some areas. Nevertheless, teachers have generally done well in introducing the National Curriculum and students appear to be benefiting from it.

Other changes in secondary education are also affecting the teacher in the classroom. Schools are now much more independent, whether grant- or LEA-maintained. They are also much more accountable, with examination results and other information being made public in league tables and inspections every four years. This has an effect on both students and teachers, and a little of it may be stimulating but too much, stressful.

The Code of Practice on the Identification and Assessment of Special Educational Needs (Department for Education 1994) has clarified the ways in which the school should deal with this area of work and has made it clear that every teacher must be involved in dealing with students with special educational needs. This also puts pressure on teachers.

Teachers are affected by the ethos of the school in which they work. All the research about effective schools suggests that clear statements of where the school is going and a more collegiate way of managing schools lead to more effective performance. Attitudes towards students by the senior staff of the school also affect the teacher in the classroom. In a school where students feel they are valued as individuals, where there are high expectations that all students can succeed if they work, where achievement of all kinds is seen to be valued by the school community, the teacher in the classroom will feel a greater sense of support in his or her work. Teachers are also supported where the school is well organized, where there are good systems supporting classroom discipline, clear rules which are widely accepted and an acceptance of the idea that to ask for support is a chance to learn, not a confession of failure.

The teacher's task will also differ according to the way the school is organized. Teaching mixed-ability classes is a different task from teaching classes which are grouped by ability, although even when there is ability grouping there will be a range of ability within the class. The task differs even more if the mixed-ability group contains students with special needs.

Schools today have to teach the National Curriculum. This is demanding but still gives a great deal of freedom to teachers to work in whatever way seems best to them. The original information about the National Curriculum suggested that there were a number of themes, skills and dimensions that schools needed to teach which were additional to the National Curriculum subjects and should be taught across the curriculum. The themes were economic understanding, careers education and guidance, environmental education, health education and citizenship. The skills were communication, numeracy, problem-solving, personal and social education, information technology and study skills. The dimensions were equal opportunities and multicultural education. These will have some relevance for you, whatever your main subject, though some themes are more relevant to some subjects than to others. Some will also be relevant to the role of the form tutor.

Underlying the way the school is organized is a set of attitudes and values which have been built up over time. Many schools are now bringing these into the open in their statements of aims and making clear the things they stand for. Whether this happens or not, the school has an ethos that is evident in the way people behave and the values they represent, in the way the staff treat each other and treat the students and the way students are encouraged to behave. You will discover these values, if they are not written down, by listening to colleagues and observing what they do. You may find that what is written down is different from what actually happens on the ground. This is called by some writers 'the hidden curriculum'. However, it is not really hidden and might be better known as 'the inferred curriculum'. There is also a hidden curriculum of things the school is teaching students which no one is really aware of. Do they, for example, get the idea that those who are not academically minded do not really count for much? Do the staff put across the message that the arts are not important or that it is better to be good at games than music and better still to be good at mathematics?

This book sets out to look at the tasks of the classroom teacher that are common to teachers in secondary schools, whatever their specialism. Each chapter looks at some aspect of classroom management and offers a checklist for the teacher to assess his or her work. Since the work of teachers is complex, it is possible to deal with some aspects of work only briefly. Each chapter therefore has suggestions for further reading which complements what has been said in the chapter.

FURTHER READING

Department of Education and Science (1987) *The New Teacher in School: a Survey by HM Inspectors in England and Wales.* London: HMSO. A report on a survey of new teachers in school.

Kyriacou, C. (1986) *Effective Teaching in Schools.* Oxford: Blackwell. Gives a full account of what is known from research to be effective in teaching.

Reid, K., Hopkins, D. and Holly, P. (1987) *Towards the Effective School.* Oxford: Blackwell. An account of what research tells us about effective schools, including effective teaching.

2

GETTING STARTED

At all stages in teaching, but particularly in your first post, your success depends to a large extent on the preparation you make. In the first place you will need to collect a good deal of information about the school. You will probably be allocated a mentor who will be an experienced teacher on the staff, and he or she will be able to help you to gather the information that you need. Much of this will be contained in the staff handbook or an equivalent collection of documents. You should also gain a good deal of information from your head of department, particularly if your mentor is not a teacher of your subject. There will be a great deal of this kind of information and you need to give some of it priority. The lists below give the information you need from the beginning.

You will be joining a team and all staff should be as helpful as possible to you, but the two people who have a special responsibility to be helpful are your mentor and your head of department. In some schools there is also a professional tutor who has overall care for student teachers and will help you with aspects of the school other than your specialist work. If you are to be a form tutor in your first post you will also be able to turn to your head of year or the person in the equivalent role for help in your tutoring role.

As a newly qualified teacher you may be included in an induction course for new teachers at the school, which will gradually introduce to you various aspects of the life and work of the school. If there are other newly qualified teachers this will give you a chance to exchange experiences and talk together about problems. There may also be meetings arranged by your LEA for newly qualified teachers, and these will also give you the opportunity to meet new teachers from other schools.

Your head of department or your mentor, if he or she is a specialist in your subject, should give you all the information you need about the working of the department, its forward planning, the resources that are available to you and the groups you will be teaching. You should be able to turn to your head of department or mentor for any problem concerning your specialism. Similarly, a newly qualified teacher who is a form tutor should be able to turn for information and help to the head of year.

Your mentor should also deal with all the more general aspects of the work, especially the various routines in the school. He or she will meet you regularly to discuss your progress. Your mentor and possibly your head of department will want to see you teach and arrange opportunities for you to see other people teach. These are positive opportunities for supporting your work in a new and highly skilled task.

The lists below give the information you will need to gather before the term starts.

What you need to know about the school
- The social background of the school.
- The layout of the school, particularly the head's room, the staff room, office, library, cloakrooms, hall, any resource centres and the rooms in which you will be teaching.
- The overall school organization, including major staff roles and responsibilities.
- The overall philosophy of the school.
- School rules.
- Relevant policies, e.g. special needs, assessment.
- Arrangements for assembly.
- The timing of the daily programme, e.g. times of breaks and lunch.
- Procedures for wet breaks and lunch.
- The timetable as it affects you.
- Whether you will be a form tutor.
- What is involved in the various staff duties.
- The school behaviour policy and discipline system, sanctions, rewards.

What you need to know about your teaching role
- The classes you will be teaching.
- The aspects of the National Curriculum and the scheme of work you will be expected to teach with each class; textbooks and other resources in use.
- The room(s) you will be using and the facilities they offer.
- Information about the previous work of each class, including something about the teaching methods employed.
- The names of the students you will be expected to teach and actual numbers in classes. Any relevant background information about them, such as those with special needs or outstanding ability.
- The records you are expected to keep of work in your classes and the assessment and marking system in use in your department.

- The arrangements for pupils entering the classroom, e.g. do they line up outside the door or come straight in?
- The seating arrangements for each class, i.e. do they normally have particular places or sit where they like?
- The resources and equipment available within the school and information about how to obtain them.
- The workbooks provided for students.
- The homework which should be set for each class.

What you need to know if you are to be a form tutor
- The responsibilities of the form tutor.
- The role and responsibilities of the head of year or equivalent post.
- The pupils who will be in your form, including any relevant information about individuals, e.g. pupils with special needs, the pronunciation of unfamiliar names.
- The records you will be expected to keep as form tutor and the reports you will have to write.
- The procedures for marking the register and other administrative tasks.
- The information you need to give to students on the first day, e.g. timetables, any notices.
- The role of the form tutor in personal and social education.
- The role of the form tutor in the discipline system.

Your working file
- Lesson notes for each day.
- Lists of each class and a note of those with special needs.
- Information about the age and ability range of each class.
- Seating plans if appropriate.
- Your timetable.
- The overall scheme of work and section of the National Curriculum within which you are working with each group.
- Your long-term or overall plans for each class you teach.

TEACHING AND LEARNING

Lesson preparation

When you first start teaching, preparing lessons takes a great deal more time than it does later, when you have experience and materials on which to draw. It is at this stage, however, that preparation really pays off. If you are well prepared you can really concentrate on your teaching.

If you are to maintain the interest of students you need to have a variety of ways into learning so that you are not always asking them to work in the same way. Every class contains students who respond to different ways of working and only by providing variety can you be sure to meet the needs of all the students in each class.

However, there is a sense in which the underlying pattern of lessons tends to be somewhat similar. Many lessons start with work on new material, a revision of what was learnt on the previous occasion or some investigation of what students already know about the topic. This is followed by work that is planned to help students make the learning their own. While students are working and at the end of the lesson you monitor how much has been learned and you may wish to end the lesson by some activity which draws the learning together. Each of these tasks can be undertaken in a variety of ways. Figure 2.1 gives a possible way of making notes for lessons which incorporates these stages and the various aspects of planning needed. You will, of course, have developed ways of making lesson notes as part of your training but the outline in Figure 2.1 is intended as a checklist for the areas in which you need to plan.

Aims and objectives

Lessons often require both aims and objectives. Aims are broad statements of intent. You may, for example, have an aim like 'To introduce students to map reading.' You may then go on to define objectives, which can be behavioural or non-behavioural. Non-behavioural objectives are not very different from aims but are more specific. In the case of map reading, a non-behavioural objective might be 'To make students aware of the function of map coordinates.' Behavioural objectives are very specific and describe what students will be able to do and under what conditions. They usually involve verbs like 'use', 'write', 'list', 'draw', 'demonstrate'. In this case you might have as a behavioural objective: 'Students will be able to use coordinates to find specific places on an ordnance survey map of the local area.'

Non-behavioural objectives are usually expressed in terms of what the teacher does, whereas behavioural objectives are expressed in terms of what the students will be able to do. The more clearly you can state both aims and objectives, the easier it will be to judge how far you are being successful in enabling students to learn. It can be helpful to think in terms of the knowledge, skills, concepts and language you want students to learn.

Having clear objectives should not prevent you from being flexible if something comes up in a lesson which you think needs attention. Your objectives are a guide to your work rather than a rigid framework.

Introduction

You may start a lesson by presenting new material, revising what was learned previously or finding out what students already know about a new topic. You may present new material yourself, ask students to read about it, use work cards, undertake field work, use videos, films or radio programmes, invite a visitor with special knowledge, or many other things. It is a good idea to share with the students your aims and objectives for the lesson so that they know where you intend them to go and what they are going to be asked to learn.

Aims and objectives				Class ___ Date ___	
	Timing	Teacher activity	Student activity	Organization	Resources
Introduction					
Consolidation/ activity					
Monitoring and evaluation					
Summing up					
Homework					

Figure 2.1 Lesson plan

New material may be introduced by investigational tasks, particularly in a subject like mathematics or science. This encourages students to use initiative and imagination in planning and conducting their investigation, and different groups may contribute differently to the learning of the whole class.

Finding out what students remember of previous work or what they know already about a new topic may involve questioning, looking at primary school records, asking students to write something about what they know, making a diagram of what they know or discussing in pairs what they know and then making a report.

The introduction to a lesson very often involves the skill of explaining things to students (see p. 69). This is a very important skill that students value in teachers and is a way of helping students to understand such things as concepts, facts, cause and effect, relationships and processes. Brown and Armstrong (1984: 123) list five basic skills in explaining:

- clarity and fluency;
- emphasis and interest;
- using examples;
- organization of the material being explained;
- feedback through opportunities for questions.

Capel *et al.* (1995: 83) make the following statement about an explanation: 'A good explanation is clear and well structured. It takes account of pupils' previous knowledge and understanding, uses language that pupils can understand, relates new work to concepts, interests or work already familiar to the pupils.'

There is also a place for students explaining things to one another. Wragg and Brown (1993: 25) suggest that:

Learning to explain a concept to another pupil, serves two important functions. The first is that the child practises clear communication and thinks about the audience, even if this is only one person; the second is that explaining to someone else can often clarify your own ideas, or reveal what it is that you do not yourself fully understand.

Some lessons will not involve the introduction of new material or revision, but they will still need some form of introduction in which you set out the work to be done.

Part of your preparation for this stage of the lesson should be the preparation of any questions you want to ask students. These may be questions about what they already know and have done that is relevant to a new topic, questions about what they have understood from your introduction or questions that make them think more deeply about the topic in question (see pp. 70–2).

Consolidation/activity

Once the lesson material has been introduced, students need to work actively on it to consolidate their learning of what has already been covered, to develop this learning further and to make it their own. It is helpful if you give students some idea of the time they have for this work so that they can learn to pace themselves. Making learning their own involves structuring what they are learning so that it can be available when it is wanted. The teacher can help students to develop structures by suggesting ways in which they might organize their learning, and with younger students it may be necessary to give a basic structure to which they can add sub-structures. Gradually they need to learn how to organize what they have learned so that it can be stored in long-term memory (see p. 45).

The most effective form of consolidation is for students to use the learning they have achieved for a real purpose. For example, work on letter writing might be followed up by writing letters to actual people, perhaps to organize a field trip. This is not always possible, however, and teachers are tempted to fall back on straightforward written work as the basic way of consolidating learning. There are many other possibilities:

- Peer tutoring involves not only the learning of new material but also the necessary consolidation of what has been learned (see pp. 32–3).
- Students might work in pairs to devise test material for the work they have been asked to learn. This will help to clarify what are the key areas to be learned, and if students know that tests will be based on the material they have devised they will concentrate on knowing the answers to the questions they set down. This is also a valuable activity in getting students to think about how to check their learning.
- Another paired task which makes absorbing the learning more interesting is to devise worksheets for other students on particular aspects of the learning that is taking place. These can deal with different aspects of the learning and may involve reading to find out more. If they are good enough they can be exchanged and used – this should be regarded as a criterion of success.
- Groups can be asked to tackle problems or look at events from a different point of view. Problem-solving is normal practice in science and mathematics, but could be used more in other subjects. Looking at events from a different point of view is particularly important in history, geography, English and religious education. Role play can be part of this work (see p. 135).
- Mastery learning involves planning the work in units and working so that everyone has to pass a test in each unit at a minimum level before proceeding to the next. Getting everyone through the tests could be set as an aim for the class, and pairs could work together to tutor and test each other, with the aim of trying to get everyone achieving high marks.
- A different approach to this might be to give students a set of test questions and ask them to learn from books or other materials with these questions in mind.
- There are a number of other possible presentation forms besides writing. A group of students can make a verbal presentation about what they have

found out from their reading, and perhaps questioning of other people. This might be on audio or video tape or live. Making a newspaper presentation might be appropriate for some work. Many teachers use display as a way of presenting what students have found out.

• Written work can be for an audience other than the teacher. For example, students might write a television script, a newspaper article or a letter to someone in a parallel group explaining what had been learned. The letters should actually be sent and the other group might reply, saying whether they think the information is accurate. Where written work is concerned, it may be a good idea to ask students to check each other's work for spelling or other language mistakes before giving it in.

Monitoring and evaluating the work

Evaluation and monitoring needs to be both formative, taking place as the lesson proceeds, and summative, assessing the outcomes of the lesson in the form of students' work. It needs to be remembered that the ability to perform a task correctly is not quite the same as having learned the thinking behind the task. You can use students' work to assess their learning, but you also need to talk to students about their work and ask questions to check whether real learning has taken place. It may be a good idea to select a small group of students in each lesson and talk with them individually in more detail about their learning, so that over a period you gradually move round the class and get a view of the level of learning from all the students. You will need to make a note about the students you have talked with as soon as possible after the lesson, so that you have a record of what you have found out.

The teacher also needs to be assessing other things as the lesson proceeds. Are students paying attention? Are they interested in the topic? Have they understood the task? Is the work at the right level for the various abilities within the class?

A very important part of evaluation is giving feedback to students, both individually and collectively. The more you can give feedback as you go along the more effective it is likely to be. This involves praising what is good as well as correcting what is inaccurate or unsatisfactory.

The various suggestions for study and presentation will require different forms of evaluation. In some cases it will be a matter of evaluating the process by which the ends have been attained as well as the final achievement. Work in pairs and groups also makes it more difficult to assess the work of individuals, since it is not easy to know how much each individual has contributed. It may therefore be necessary to assess on a group or paired basis.

Written work provides a means of diagnosing difficulties. For example, if you collect the spelling mistakes of a student who has a weakness in this direction, you can very often see the mistakes in his or her thinking which lead to the spelling mistakes. There will be students who have difficulty in knowing when to double a letter in the middle of a word which has a suffix. The rule for this is that you double the letter if the vowel in the first part of the word is short – 'a' as in apple rather than long like 'a' as in pane. Thus 'mating' has only one 't' and 'matting' two. If you identify mistakes which recur you may be able to suggest ways of helping the student. Every aspect of teaching should be diagnostic.

You may decide that you want to test what students have learned, and the test will need to be prepared in advance. You may like from time to time to give students an evaluation sheet to give their views about a topic as it reaches completion. This can ask them to assess how well they think they did on particular work, parts where they felt they did not understand and need to do further work and comments on any particular aspects of the work they enjoyed. This gives you a lot of useful information and is valuable for the students in helping them to identify what they still need to learn. It can also be helpful in planning new work.

You still need to reflect on what has happened yourself. It is very easy to be so concerned with planning the next day's lessons that you do not take time to reflect on what has happened today. Yet this is important for your learning. It may be helpful to list the things that went well and those that did not go so well, and to consider how you will build on those that went well and improve on those which did not. It is also useful to ask yourself what students actually learned.

Newman (1990) points out that there is often a difference between what teachers say they believe and what they actually do in the classroom. There is a need to make one's beliefs explicit and look at one's practice in the light of them. Your beliefs about education will probably change as you become more experienced and talk to other teachers, but you need, nevertheless, to think about what you believe.

Most lessons and the following homework will produce work that needs to be marked. The process of grading or marking should be part of the school or department policy on assessment, but the comments you make are in many ways more important for students' learning. They should be as positive as possible, praising what is good and giving pointers for ways of improving the work. You also need to decide what should be recorded about the work. Simply recording marks or grades tells you a very limited amount about the work a student has done. You need to find a way of recording any comments you may have about students from time to time. It is also helpful if you at least occasionally record the comments you have put on students' work. This gives you much better information for writing reports than simply a list of marks.

Marking is a very time-consuming part of the teacher's work and it can be made a little easier if you have exercise books given in open at the page that needs marking. It also helps if you insist that students date each piece of work, so that it is clear which piece of work needs marking.

Producing an essay on what has been learned is a fairly standard procedure. It can be interesting to ask older students to give in their essays or other work with a mark attached and with a justification for that mark. A variation on this is to discuss criteria for marking essays or other work and then allow pairs or trios to mark each other's work using the agreed criteria. This will need checking by the teacher but it is valuable in helping students to see what is being sought.

Summing up

At the end of the lesson you may want to draw together what has been learned, so that students go away with a clear idea of the work they have covered. This is not essential but is sometimes helpful. You may do this by summing up the work that has been done yourself, but it may be better to ask questions that enable students to sum up their learning. These questions should be prepared in advance. This then becomes part of the monitoring of the learning that has taken place, and gives you a starting point for the next lesson.

Homework

Homework should ideally grow out of the work in the classroom, and it is important that you give very clear instructions about it because students cannot ask you about it when they set to work at home.

Resources

In preparing for a lesson you need to think carefully about the resources you will need. Are you planning to use the overhead projector? If so, have you either transparencies which are already prepared or transparencies and pens to use in the classroom. Transparencies need to be clear and uncluttered. If you are using a word processor to produce them you need at least 18 point print. If you are producing handwritten transparencies it is a good idea to use water soluble pens so that you can make changes if you want to use the same transparencies again. It also helps to place a sheet of widely spaced lined paper under the transparency while you are making it, so that you keep your writing in straight lines. Remember to adjust the projector before the lesson so that it is focused and ready to use when you want it.

If you are planning to use slides you need to be sure that the projector is in place and working and that your slides are in the order you want them. Where you plan to use a video, make sure you know how to work the video recorder and the television set. If some students will be using a computer you need to be sure that you have the right software and are knowledgeable about how to get the programme started. It pays to give some thought to what you will do if any of the equipment goes wrong so that you can't use it.

You may want students to use resources of various kinds, and in this case you need to think out in advance where you will put them and what sorts of rules you will make for their use.

Checklist 1 – Lesson preparation

- Am I clear about my objectives for the lesson?
- Do I know what knowledge and experience students already have on this topic?
- Have I planned the introduction to the work?
- Have I planned the questions I want to ask?
- Am I clear about the activities the students will be carrying out?
- Have I planned how I am going to set these in action?
- Have I catered for all abilities?
- Have I material for those who finish early?
- Have I all the material and resources I need and checked that they are ready for use?
- What monitoring activities shall I be carrying out?
- How am I going to finish the lesson?
- Have I planned the homework that will be needed?

MANAGING LEARNING

In addition to preparing the actual material you want students to learn, you need to have clear ideas of what you intend to do about various aspects of classroom organization. You need to consider the following points.

Are you going to allow students to choose where they sit? If you have information from other teachers about the normal pattern you may be guided by this, but since you have the task of learning names as quickly as possible it is important that students stay in the same seat from lesson to lesson unless you move them. This means that if you decide to let them choose seats you will need to make a note of who is sitting where, and this may be difficult to do while you have other teaching tasks. You can overcome this problem by asking a student to do this for you or find out individual names while the students undertake a task you have given them. Have plans of the classroom drawn up ready to insert names.

Alternatively, you can plan the seating and insist that students sit in, for example, alphabetical order. This also avoids all the trouble makers aiming for the back of the classroom. You also need to avoid having boys and girls sitting in large separate groups, since when this happens, it is easy to pay more attention to the boys than the girls because they are often more demanding.

If you decide to let students sit where they wish, make it clear that you have decided this and that you have the right to move people if they behave badly in the places they have chosen. In other words, you need to emphasize that you are in control.

It is wise to check each lesson on the students who are present, and they need some work to do while you are doing this. It is important that they know you check, even if you do it informally as they are working. You may need to take up the question of absences with the form tutor.

If students come into the classroom as they arrive rather than lining up outside, have something interesting prepared for them to do as soon as they come in, so that they don't sit waiting for the whole class to gather with nothing to do. This can be on an overhead projector, which enables you to keep the transparencies for future use. It might be a puzzle or an opportunity to get students to note what they remember of the last lesson or what they know about or have experienced relevant to a new topic. You can also use this kind of short interesting activity while you are settling students into places and making a map of who is sitting where. In the longer term you may train them to start on particular aspects of their work as soon as they come in.

It is also useful to have some filler type activities for times at the end of a lesson when the clearing up has gone well and everyone is ready to go but there are still a few minutes left. These need to be rather different – activities the class does with you rather than individually. You might, for example, talk about the work which will be coming up in the next few lessons and ask questions to discover what students already know about it; you might ask questions about the work which has been studied in the lesson finishing; you could also check on whether students know the language you want to use in the next few lessons or check on their understanding of any new words introduced in the current lesson.

If you have things to give out, think about how you will do this. If everyone has to have a copy of the same material, you can give it out by passing it around or by giving it out yourself while students are doing something else. If you are returning work you may want to comment to individuals. This is probably best done by giving out the work while the students are occupied with something else. It is useful while you are learning names to give back work individually. This helps you with matching names to faces. This also enables you to talk to individuals where appropriate and to give a word of praise where it seems useful. Establish a routine for this kind of activity.

Think out carefully the points in the lesson when you want to change activities. If what you plan involves moving students or furniture, work out exactly how you intend this to be done and insist that no one moves until you have given all the instructions and said that movement can start. You will also need to think out how you will return the students and the furniture to their original places at the end of the lesson.

List the resources you will need, check where each of them can be found and make sure you have collected them well before the lesson in which you need them. You also need to think about how you get students started on work which involves the individual use of different resources. Waterhouse (1983) suggests that one way of doing this is to give everyone the same short task and then give out work cards while students are working at this. They will finish the original task at different times and can start on the individual tasks as they finish. This will avoid queues for the resources.

Decide whether you need to write on the board and plan how you will lay out your material. It is best not to have lines which are too long, and do your best to keep these straight. If you are writing up ideas from students put these in columns so that they look tidy, remembering that you are setting an example for your students. Do not try to talk to the class while you are writing on the board. You may find it best if you stand sideways to the board and turn to scan the class every so often. If you use the board, don't forget to see that it is cleaned before you leave the room.

If you know what you want to put up it may be better to use the overhead projector. Then you can make your transparencies in advance and keep your eyes on the students when you present the material. You can also file and keep the transparencies.

Consider whether the work you plan contributes towards the students becoming independent learners. Does it develop critical thinking? Help students to develop concepts? Make generalizations? Apply knowledge to new situations?

Decide whether you want students to help each other. In the first instance it is probably better to follow what is normally done in the particular classes you teach. If you wish to encourage peer group help where it has not been previous practice, do it gradually.

Have a routine for what students are expected to do when they have finished

Checklist 2 – Management planning

- Have I decided what to do about seating arrangements?
- Have I planned 'filler' activities in case I need them at the beginning and end of the lesson?
- Do I know how I am going to organize changes of activity?
- Have I all the resources I need for the lesson?
- Have I planned how the resources are to be used?
- Am I planning anything that will help students to become independent learners?
- Shall I allow/encourage students to help each other?
- What should students do when they have finished?
- Have I considered what might go wrong?
- Are there any safety issues I should consider?

a piece of work. There should always be some interesting work which they can pick up so that they do not waste time. It can be a waste of student time for them to do more of the same work if they have already mastered it.

Consider the things that may go wrong. Students may come without their books, without paper or writing tools. There could be interruptions. Some students may finish early. Work out how you will deal with these eventualities.

Consider whether there are any safety issues. This will vary from one subject to another, but it is important to be prepared for activities which could be dangerous if they are not well handled.

Think out how you will end each lesson. Ideally you need to give some kind of summary of what has been learned. There may be homework to be set. You then need routines for collecting work, returning resource material to the right places and clearing up generally. You may need to warn students of things they will need to bring for the next lesson and you would be wise to get them to write this down. You also need to think about the way students will leave the room.

Long-term planning

As a newly qualified teacher you will need to make plans for at least a term, and broad plans for the whole year. These will be governed to some extent by the National Curriculum and departmental planning, but you need your own plan. The following steps may be useful:

- Take the department plan for each class you teach and break it up into sections dealing with the different topics which you think will make a coherent programme. Ideally, one topic needs to lead logically on to another, though this is not always possible. Put dates for the lessons for each section. You may have difficulty in keeping to these but you need them as a guide. It is not easy when one starts teaching to assess how much can be covered in one lesson or group of lessons, but one gradually becomes able to assess this more accurately. If you attempt to make judgements about this in your planning you will be able to see how accurate your assessment was, and this will enable you to improve on your judgement of how much you can cover next time.

- Work out a broad plan for each topic, stating aims and objectives clearly in each case. It may be helpful to think in terms of the knowledge, skills, concepts and language you want students to acquire.

- Look at issues like the resources you will need and any field work or visits you will want to make.

- Find out the school arrangements for field work and visits and start to make any necessary arrangements in good time.

- Check on what is available in the school by way of resources for the topics you will be doing first, and make a point of checking well in advance for each of the subsequent topics.

- Find out how to order any resources not in the school and order them in good time.
- Allow yourself time for making worksheets or task cards and for preparing resources and audio-visual aids for use.
- Consider for each topic:
  how you will find out what has been taught before and what students know already;
  how you will introduce the topic;
  what you may need to provide by way of work cards and audio-visual aids;
  the work you may need to do to prepare the resources for student use;
  how you will enable the students to make the learning their own by doing and discussion;
  how you will assess what has been learned;
  what you will set for homework.
- Consider how you will evaluate the whole programme.

FURTHER READING

Capel, S., Leask, M. and Turner, T. (1995) *Learning to Teach in the Secondary School: a Companion to School Experience.* London: Routledge. Written with student teachers in mind but gives practical help on many aspects of teaching. Gives a useful account of long-term planning.

Cohen, L. and Manion, L. (1989) *A Guide to Teaching Practice*, 3rd. edn. London: Routledge. Written mainly with student teachers in mind but with valuable advice for newly qualified teachers.

Hull, J. (1990) *Classroom Skills – a Teachers' Guide.* London: David Fulton. A book mainly for beginning teachers which gives useful information on all aspects of teaching.

Marland, M. (1975) *The Craft of the Classroom: a Survival Guide.* London: Heinemann. A very practical account of the teacher's work, with suggestions about how to deal with many of the day-to-day problems of teaching.

Waterhouse, P. (1983) *Managing the Learning Process.* Maidenhead: McGraw-Hill. Particularly helpful material on planning.

Wragg, E.C. (1984) *Classroom Teaching Skills.* London: Croom Helm/Routledge. A presentation of research findings on classroom teaching which have practical application.

3

THE STUDENTS

THE DEVELOPMENT OF YOUNG PEOPLE

The better you know your students, the more able you become to match work to individual student needs. The more you know about the way children and young people develop, the more easily you recognize some of the problems students find in learning. Hull (1990: 36) makes the point that 'It is only when you are aware of the stage of development below the ages of those you teach, that you will recognise more easily those children who are immature and functioning either emotionally or intellectually below the majority of their peers.' The good teacher takes every opportunity to get to know students, talking to them outside the classroom and getting to know their background and interests as well as working with them in the classroom.

The period of secondary schooling is for many young people a difficult time. Some have already entered puberty before they enter the secondary school, and the number of these increases slightly year by year. Others take longer to develop, but all of them have to cope with not only a period of rapid growth but also the hormonal and emotional changes this brings with it. These changes are not made easier by the fact that our society, unlike some more primitive cultures, has no way of marking the fact that the boy has become a man and the girl a woman. We have various ages at which certain adult activities are permissible. Marrying, voting and driving are all allowed at different ages, and there is no school leaving ceremony comparable to American graduation. As Mussen *et al.* (1963: 507) point out, 'The adolescent has renounced childhood, but has not yet been fully accepted as an adult.' At the same time the young person is beginning to identify with the adult world and in the process of

Case study 1

Robert was about average in size when he entered the secondary school but he started to shoot up in year 8, and by the time he was in year 9 he was almost of adult size. He found this very disconcerting. He became clumsy and seemed too big for school furniture. He also found it very difficult to get himself organized and his form tutor was frequently receiving complaints about him from colleagues, because he never had the right things for lessons. She talked this over with him and got him to write a list of the things he needed each day in the week, so that he could check each evening whether he had the right things ready. She also did her best to check this with him each morning, and when she met his parents at a parents' evening she explained what she had done and asked them to check each day that he had the right things on his list for the day. Complaints gradually became fewer, though he still forgot things from time to time, but he gradually got into the habit of checking.

establishing a personal identity and a new sort of relationship with adults, particularly with parents.

The physical and emotional changes bring their own difficulties. Children quickly become physically young men and young women but take time to come to terms with their physical selves and to acquire the behaviour expected of their changed status. Girls develop more quickly than boys and the boys catch up later. Recent studies of the achievements of boys and girls show girls doing better than boys in many areas of the curriculum, and this is something to which many schools are now giving attention.

Hamblin (1974: 6) describes the problem of adolescence as follows:

The identity crisis occurs during the earlier years of adolescence when the child is separating himself socially and emotionally from dependence upon his parents. He begins to build up a new social, vocational and sexual self, but this causes strain. Early adolescence is a period of storm and stress in some pupils because the boy or girl is uncertain. He adopts trial roles in a clumsy and exaggerated way. At the same time he is vulnerable to criticism and attack, not only from adults but from friends of his own age.

Schools have the difficult task of working with young people, some of whom look like adults when they may feel like children inside and behave like children from time to time. This is rendered even more difficult for the teacher by the fact that different people mature at different stages, and any class in the lower part of the secondary school will contain some students who look and behave like children, some who look like adults and behave like children and some who look like adults and are beginning to behave in a more mature way. They are very conscious of their bodies at this stage, and both those who have

Case study 2

Janice was smaller than her contemporaries when she entered year 9 and had still not started to develop. She found this very worrying and it started to affect her work. She was very good at games and was in the school team for netball in spite of her youth. She had a good relationship with the physical education teacher and one day when they were on the way to a match the teacher commented on Janice's good play, adding that her small size seemed to make her more mobile. This created an opportunity for Janice to express her worries about her lack of development. The teacher was able to reassure her that some people were slower to develop than others but development was inevitable and only a matter of time. Janice found this comforting and was glad to have shared her worry with someone else.

matured early and those who are late in maturing find this a cause for concern. The more the school is able to treat young people as adults the more they are likely to learn to behave as adults. There are considerable advantages in admitting adults to sixth form classes, where they serve as role models for the young people.

Davis (1985) made a study of how young people were reacting to various aspects of their lives at home and at school, and he makes the following comments about their development:

> For a considerable number of pupils a marked shift would appear to have taken place during the period covered by the summer term at the end of the third year and the long vacation before the fourth year in their understanding of themselves and in their ability to make a rational analysis of their behaviour and relationships. For some pupils a whole, deeply satisfying world was revealed as they gained control of elements of their lives and gave shape to parts of their emotional selves in a way previously inaccessible by virtue of the constraints of childhood; even the accompanying pain and depression of adolescence was accepted as complementary to the process and to an extent 'enjoyed'.
>
> (Davis 1985: 63)

Adolescents are gradually developing as people, and part of this development is an understanding of self. They become increasingly self-conscious and self-critical during adolescence, and this is not made easier by the changes in physical development. They are also concerned about developing social relationships. The peer group becomes increasingly important; the views of their friends affect the development of self-esteem and individuals seek prestige in the eyes of their contemporaries. Form tutors may have to contend with group rivalries within the class.

In today's society many young people are having to cope with family break-up and this can be a form of bereavement as the boy or girl gradually comes to terms with the fact that one of his or her parents is no longer in the home. This may have been preceded by quarrelling and violence which also posed problems for the young person.

Young people are also the targets of the commercial world, which sees them as a separate market with money to spend. The desire for peer acceptance and to be like one's peers is strong at this stage and this influences buying. School can do much to help young people to become better judges of whether what they buy is good value for money.

School is also concerned with the values that young people are developing. Most schools are concerned to encourage such values as hard work, thoughtfulness towards others, honesty and politeness. Some schools are now making statements of the values they stand for, and you may have such a statement to support your own attempts to put values before those you teach. Whether this kind of support exists or not and whether you think through the values you believe in or not, your own values will be evident to students in what you say and do. It is worth thinking about this and what you would wish to put across.

Students in secondary schools experience a growing interest in sex, and research suggests that some 16 per cent will have experienced sexual intercourse before they leave school, often with no protection. Sex education and education about HIV is of considerable importance at the secondary stage, as is education about drugs.

A study by Graham (1994) looked at a sample of boys and girls on the three indices of satisfaction, commitment to school and attitudes to teachers. He found a steady decline in all three areas from year 7, with levels increasing slightly or levelling out in years 10 and 11. Students said that in year 7 success came easily and teachers were very careful to reward it. In year 8 the work got harder and at the same time the teachers got less supportive. The nearness of examinations probably accounted for the levelling out or improvement in years 10 and 11. This was only a small sample in four schools, and may not be more widely representative, but it would seem to accord with the views of teachers.

Waterhouse (1983: 102) notes that as students mature intellectually, 'different styles of reasoning will begin to emerge: comparing and contrasting, looking for cause–effect relationships; speculative thinking, deductive thinking.' These styles of thinking require encouragement on the part of the teacher if they are to be used to good effect.

The development of the self-image

A very important part of development is the formation of the self-image. Students will enter the secondary school with a picture of themselves gained from their years in the primary school and from home and peer group, and these views will affect the way they see the curricular programme on offer. It is important for the school and for individual teachers to take seriously the need for students to develop a good self-image, one that says 'I can, and I am in control of my own success and failure', rather than a more negative view which sees life as something over which one has no control.

The whole of the time in school contributes to the self-image. A casual comment by the teacher or by a friend may affect it. Praise for work well done and for good learning and behaviour obviously contributes, and it is therefore important that every student receives appropriate praise. It is the teacher's task to see that work is sufficiently well matched to each student so that it is possible genuinely to praise each person and help to build his or her self-esteem. This is, of course, a counsel of perfection, but one which all teachers should bear in mind. Casual negative comments have the reverse effect. Where work and behaviour are not good, comment can still be in positive terms, implying that the teacher believes that the student in question is capable of good work and behaviour but is not performing to his or her ability level. Students need to feel supported and competent and the teacher can help this by treating students as responsible people and helping them to set realistic goals and evaluate themselves intelligently, giving recognition to their good points as well as recognizing their weaknesses.

Students praise and criticize one another informally and this is also a contribution to learning. They are building up pictures of themselves as being good at this and bad at that, able to get on well with other people or having problems in getting on with other people and so on. By the time they leave the primary school they are already confident in their ability to do some things and worried about their performance in others. The secondary school offers a new start where good teachers can change attitudes for some students.

Young people's self-images are reflected in the way they relate to others. A student with a poor self-image will expect others to respond negatively and will often create this reaction by behaving provocatively. School can help by teaching social skills. A form tutor may be able to help individual students who seem to have difficulty in getting on with their peers by suggesting ways in which they could improve their social relationships.

Parsons *et al.* (1976) found that girls tended to assess their abilities as being lower than they were in actuality. Girls were more worried about failure and more sensitive to negative information, and this was evident from the age of about four. Girls tend to have lower self-esteem than boys, perhaps reflecting the role of women in society.

The development of the self-image is closely related to the expectation of others for the progress of students. If the students' parents or teachers demonstrate that they have high expectations of them, there is more likelihood that those students will achieve, providing that the high expectations are ones which the students are able to fulfil. They are then reinforced by success and start the next task with increased confidence. However, there is also the complementary problem that parents and teachers can pressure young people with their expectations, so that they eventually give up trying because they do not think they can live up to such expectations.

Alternatively the expectations of others can give rise to an increasingly negative cycle in which the student fails, the teacher lowers expectation and the student's self-image is diminished correspondingly. Or the demonstration of low expectations can lead to low levels of achievement. The teacher's professional task is to get the level of expectation high enough to challenge and encourage, but within each student's capacity.

Edwards and Mercer (1987) suggest that failure is too often seen as the property of students, whereas it may be the outcome of the communicative process. What is needed is more effective structuring of what is to be learned and an approach which recognizes that teaching does not necessarily result in learning. Each student has to learn for himself or herself. The teacher has to find ways of enabling learning to take place.

There is research evidence to suggest that teachers underestimate some children within the class and overestimate others. The study by Mortimore *et al.* (1988) of Inner London primary schools found that the teachers studied tended to underestimate the younger children in the class, often because they were not really aware of the differences in ages. They also tended to overestimate the boys compared with the girls. This is a study of primary school children and may not necessarily apply at the secondary level, but teachers in secondary schools need to consider whether they are aware of which are the younger children in each class and consider whether they are underestimating them. Sharp (1995) found that summer born children, who will always be the youngest in their classes, continue to do less well throughout schooling even at GSCE and A level.

Teachers need to be conscious of their views of the performance of boys and girls. Other studies have found that teachers tend to underestimate children from working-class homes and black students. Well-behaved children who work well tend to be overestimated.

The development of the self-image is closely bound up with the physical, social and emotional development of the child. Part of the self-image will concern the student's physical appearance. Young people are sensitive about this at adolescence and students such as Robert and Janice, described earlier in this chapter, find that their development affects their confidence, social development and the way in which they learn to cope with personal feelings and reactions. Teachers need to be sensitive to this and try to help individuals to cope with the way others treat them, and at the same time encouraging young people to be sensitive and supportive to each other.

LEARNING

The teacher's task is to enable students to learn. Teaching and learning are not the same. A teacher can apparently teach something, only to discover that students have learned comparatively little. Only the student can learn.

'Learning only becomes meaningful when the learner has integrated it into what he already knows' (Sutton 1981: 4). It then becomes linked to other learning, which makes it easier to recall. It is part of the teacher's task to help students to integrate new learning.

Bruner (1966) speaks of learning as a search for patterns, regularities and predictability. Capel *et al.* (1995: 221, 222) point out that 'one aspect of the teacher's role is to assist pupils in the formulation and discovery of such patterns and rules – thus enhancing and expanding their knowledge.' They also note that 'Knowledge is not "out there" but is personally and socially constructed. It may be evaluated by individuals to the extent to which it fits their experience and is coherent with other aspects of knowledge.'

Kyriacou (1986: 34) suggests that 'Pupil learning can be defined as changes in a pupil's behaviour which take place as a result of being engaged in an educational experience.' This tends to imply that learning is an intentional process and that educational experiences are different from other experiences. In reality, some of the most important learning takes place incidentally and without the student being aware of it. Young people use others, both adults and other young people, as models, for example, and changes in their behaviour take place as a result of attempts to imitate the behaviour of the models. Changes in behaviour in young people also take place as a result of the reaction of others to them and in many other situations. Not all of this learning is desirable. Young people may admire and use as models people about whom their parents and teachers would feel concern. They may be led astray by the reactions of others. The intentional process of learning may need to combat other undesirable learning.

Learning is an extremely complex process and different people have different styles of learning. Some students learn easily from the words of the teacher and from books. Others need more practical experience. Learning is more likely to take place where the student is in a problem-solving situation that stimulates and challenges. There is also evidence that students learn well when they work cooperatively in groups with others. This provides an opportunity for them to talk about what they are learning and helps them to make the learning their own. Teachers need to use a variety of strategies to cater for the various learning styles in their classes.

The development that takes place in young people in the secondary school years is not only physical and emotional. There are also cognitive differences. Many move from Piaget's 'concrete operational' stage to the stage of abstract learning. On entry to secondary school, some children will already have the ability to think in abstract ways while others will still be thinking in concrete terms in some areas by the time they leave school and beyond. People generally are able to think in abstract ways in some areas but need concrete examples in others. This poses considerable problems for teachers, particularly if groups are of mixed ability. The students who are still at the concrete operational stage require much more first-hand experience than those who have learned to think abstractly. However, first-hand experience in which the teacher brings things into the classroom or takes students out for field work is stimulating for all students and so contributes to learning for everyone. Piaget and Inhelder (1969) make the point that learning initially concerns short-term memory. The learner then processes the information into what they call *schemas* in long-term memory. In effect this means that the student has to structure what he or she learns in order to store it and have it available when it is necessary to recall it. The teacher can help with the structuring process by encouraging students to classify what they are learning in various ways. Sometimes this will emerge naturally from the nature of the material being learned, but on other occasions students need to set up a structure in order to remember something (see p. 61). This is all part of the process of becoming an independent learner.

Bruner (1968) describes the learning experience as making a model of the world in the mind. He lists three ways in which we represent experience to ourselves:

- enactive, based on knowledge from physical action;
- iconic, based on knowledge derived from forming and organizing images;
- symbolic, based on knowledge derived from the use of language in terms of words or other symbols.

When you are planning learning it is important to remember that words mean only as much as the experience the learners bring to them. When you are planning new work with a group, it is a good idea to consider what language you want to use and what experience students will need to have full understanding of the language. Sometimes this will be a matter of questioning to find out whether the words and expressions you want to use are familiar, and sometimes it will be more a matter of providing explanations and practical experience. You also need to consider whether students are able to use the language you need but may be giving it more limited meaning than you would wish. The younger and less able the students, the more important it is to give consideration to language.

Another important set of relationships to consider is that of intelligence, experience and language. We very often underestimate the intelligence of young people and overestimate their experience. Language development is one of the most important areas of work for the teacher, whatever the subject, and is rightly regarded as a cornerstone of each student's education. The ability to use language determines not only the nature of a person's relationships with others and the ability to cooperate but also, to some extent, the ability to think, since language is the medium of a good deal of human thought. Each subject has its own way of using language and its own vocabulary and use of words. To think like a historian or a scientist you need the language of those subjects. Students also need the opportunity to use the subject language in their own discussion, rather than merely listening to it.

It is not only important to know what experiences and language the students have when you start a new piece of work. You also need to remember that they will probably have ideas about it, which may affect their ability to take in the new work. This is particularly true in science, where students often have erroneous ideas of why things happen and are not always convinced by the experimental work they do. You need to start where the students are in their thinking, and this means paying attention to finding out their ideas. It may be helpful when starting new work to build up a chart on the board of the things that students already know about the work you want to do. You can start this by writing a keyword in the middle of the board and then adding ideas that come from students, linking them with arrows to the keyword and to each other.

Vygotsky (1978) suggests that children and young people undergo quite profound changes in their understanding by engaging in joint activity and conversation with other people. This is also noted by Bennett (1992: 10), who makes the following points:

> What the body of research into children's conceptions, or 'alternative frameworks' has shown is that they often hold unorthodox conceptions about a wide range of topics taught in school; that these conceptions shape how they make sense of new information, thereby often exacerbating learning difficulties; and that learners often find it difficult to modify their conceptions, particularly in areas like science, where they prefer to hold on to their intuitive ideas.

He goes on to suggest that one way in which these unorthodox views are modified is through discussion, and that it is necessary for students to discuss what they are learning with others in order to sort out their thinking and structure it. He is here talking about primary school children, but the principle applies more strongly to the secondary school, in that students have formed much firmer views about things by this stage.

Language is the main medium by which children learn. Edwards and Mercer (1987) describe the way in which teachers have to work to achieve common understanding in the language used in the classroom. They stress the importance of classroom talk as a means of learning, and suggest that what is needed is sharing, comparing, contrasting and arguing perspectives against those of others. They also stress the need for students to reflect on what is being learned.

Vygotsky (1986) writes of the *zone of proximal development*, by which he means the gap between what the learner can do independently and what he or she can do with help from someone else. The teacher operates in this zone and it is here that learning is gradually extended.

Written work helps students to make learning their own. It does this most effectively when there is an opportunity for them to write fairly freely. With younger students in particular it is helpful in subjects such as history, geography and religious education if they can put themselves in the position of people in the place or period being studied and write in the first person. There is also a case for using devices which require writing for someone other than the teacher. Newspaper accounts, letters, stories, diaries, television scripts, profiles of people, obituaries, crime reports and so on make good alternatives. If any of these can in some sense be used or published, this gives a reality to the work. Thus one history group might exchange letters or stories with another group about what they have learned about a particular topic. Students need to interpret the knowledge they are gaining for themselves, and writing about it is one way to do this.

MOTIVATION

As a teacher you need to be concerned with what motivates students to learn. Sumner (1987: 46,47) looked at ways of testing motivation and identified the following as motivators:

- reward, response to tokens and praise/sanctions;
- intellectual, urge to extend understanding;
- enjoyment, school work that is appealing and amusing in content and activity;
- sociability, work done in collaboration with others or in company with others;
- status, opportunity to gain approval from peers or relevant adults;
- self-realization, development and enhancement of self-concept.

Motivation may be intrinsic or extrinsic. Intrinsic motivation stems from needs within the person – a strong interest in the material being studied, for example. Extrinsic motivation comes from without. A student works to achieve good marks, examination success, approbation by parents and teachers and so on. There are elements of both of these affecting every student.

Skinner (1968) writes of operant conditioning. Behaviour and work that is reinforced by praise from the teacher or appreciation from peers is likely to be repeated. Undesirable behaviour may be decreased by the absence of reinforcement, by punishment and response costs or by the removal of expected rewards.

Fontana (1994: 99) suggests that students are likely to be motivated if the work seems relevant and 'helps them in some way to make a success of their lives'. He includes here not only work which helps students to prepare for future careers but also work which helps them to relate well to others, skills for mastering the physical environment, helping them to recognize their own abilities and develop them and helping them to 'accept and value themselves as individuals and ultimately to help them see a meaning and purpose in their own and other people's existence.' He also points out that students will vary in what they see as relevant.

Students are more likely to be motivated if they feel they have some control over events. This means involving them from time to time in planning how a piece of work might be carried out, giving them responsibility occasionally for deciding on the end product of a piece of work, sometimes involving them in assessing their own work and that of their peers and generally discussing with them how best to learn the material under consideration.

Part of your task as teacher is to find ways of motivating all the students in the group. This is most likely to happen when teacher and students share clearly defined common goals and can see ways of achieving them.

There follows a review of the ways in which people can be motivated. It may be useful, when you are deciding what to do about a particular student or group, to review the list, considering the possibilities in relation to the problem in question.

Inner need. Human beings are motivated by inner needs. Where a student is motivated by an inner need, there appears to be a greater power for learning. There will be some young people in the groups you teach who are motivated by a need to succeed in everything they do. This has disadvantages as well as advantages, in that they are discouraged by failure and find it difficult to see that failure is also a means of learning. Very able students are often in this category.

There will be others whose inner need leads them in a quite different direction. Some will hope to impress their peer group by baiting the teacher and generally showing difficult behaviour. Punishment will reinforce the impression of toughness they wish to create. Such students need to be identified and encouraged to develop other behaviour patterns early in their school careers.

Recognition and praise. It is very important that young people feel that they are known and valued as individuals. Hamblin (1978: 27) quotes a boy as saying: 'It is halfway through the first term and only four teachers know my name and that's not including my form tutor, he don't know my name yet. I say if they don't know you, they can't help you.' A student who has this kind of experience may well look to the peer group for recognition and become one of the more difficult students. Capel *et al.* (1995: 105) comment: 'Pupils need to feel that they are individuals, with their needs and interests taken into account, rather than being a member of a group.'

Praise is very important to us all and teachers need to look for ways of giving genuine praise to all students from time to time for behaviour as well as work. It is wise to try to think of different ways of working expressions of praise. If you always make the same comments they tend to lose their value.

First-hand experience. Seeing and doing for oneself is motivating, and it is important for students' development in all aspects of their work that they have a good deal of first-hand experience, handling and using materials and undertaking field work of various kinds. This enables them to see the application of what they are learning and is therefore motivating. It is also important for language development, since in this context language acquires genuine meaning.

A desire for mastery or a problem that is challenging. Problem-solving or mastering a skill is an enjoyable human activity, as may be seen from the popularity of crosswords and other puzzles and games of skill, and particularly from young peoples' enthusiasm for computer games. Part of your task as a teacher is to offer your students opportunities to work out ideas and tackle problems within their capacity. For example, a question that students could profitably study in both history and geography is why a town grew up in a particular place. This involves considering what towns have offered to people in the past and the present and what towns need to survive, and leads to much important learning. Mastering a skill is also motivating, and computers offer a particular challenge to most young people.

Increasing independence. Where students have some control over their learning, either in the way they set about the learning task or in the end product required, this fosters self-confidence and increases interest, and is therefore motivating.

Competition. Human beings are naturally competitive, and most teachers use this to some extent. Even if the teacher avoids competitive situations, the students are inclined to make comparisons. The trouble about competition is that a student may place too much emphasis on winning, getting a good mark or whatever the reward may be, and too little on the learning itself. The second difficulty is that some tend to be losers every time, and this is not good for their self-image and consequent attitude to work. Nevertheless, competition is useful, especially if it can be a matter of beating your own previous performance or vying with someone of comparable ability. In short, competition can be motivating but needs to be used with care.

Self-improvement. A person who has clear goals is more likely to succeed than someone with little sense of direction. If you can help students to identify their own sets of short-term targets, their natural desire for improvement may support their learning. It is also a good idea to suggest that students use friends to help them to check how they are doing in achieving their targets.

Many students in years 10 and 11 and also in the sixth form will be motivated by examinations and the need to obtain qualifications leading to employment or higher education. There are likely to be differences according to background, in that some students will have been brought up to recognize the importance of deferring satisfaction and will see the importance for future employment of succeeding at school. Others will not have this advantage and will need a lot of persuasion and support to see the importance of working hard at school.

Cooperation. There is a satisfaction in working as part of a group and a degree of pressure to contribute which can motivate some young people. It is also important as a means of learning how to work with a group, which is a very necessary skill for adult life. This should be made clear to students, who sometimes see group work as a soft option.

Teaching someone else. This can be a valuable way of working for everyone involved, because the 'teacher' has to learn and then get another person to learn. The student doing the teaching reinforces his or her own knowledge in the process of helping someone else. Goodlad and Hirst (1990: 9) state that qualitative reports on peer tutoring show that there are gains in improving attitude, behaviour and self-esteem of tutors. They also state that 'Tutees have much to gain; they are provided with a companion involved in their learning who shows interest in their work and is more available to praise their success.' This is discussed further in Chapter 5.

The use of appropriate equipment. There is no doubt that equipment which 'does' something is motivating. Given appropriate software, students can learn a great deal from computers with very little help from the teacher. Computers have something to contribute to learning in every subject, and teachers need to make good use of whatever opportunities the school can offer.

EQUAL OPPORTUNITIES

The school will have a policy for equal opportunities, but it is up to every teacher to see that there is equality in the way students are treated in class and about the school. There is still a great deal of evidence of inequality in the areas of gender, race, social background and ability, and in other ways too. For example, Crane and Mellon (1978) found that teachers tended to think that well-behaved children had a higher academic potential than those who were less well-behaved. Galton and Delafield (1981) found that there was a tendency for children for whom the teacher had high expectation to receive more praise and more contact with the teacher than low achievers who not only received less praise, but less feedback on their work. Tizard *et al.* (1988) found that among primary children boys generally received more criticism than girls and more praise, and black boys received most criticism and disapproval and white girls least criticism and least praise. Secondary school teachers need to check whether this is also true at the later stages of education. Hamblin (1978) noted that it was very easy for teachers to reinforce a negative view for some students. Where a young person built a reputation for being difficult, teachers began to expect trouble and to reinforce the trouble maker's reputation by their behaviour, rarely praising and frequently making negative comments.

Gender

There is evidence that teachers treat boys and girls differently, usually to the detriment of girls. There is also the fact that girls and boys demonstrate different abilities and interests and perform differently in examinations. Boys still tend to do better than girls at mathematics and science, although girls are catching up and girls do better than boys at languages and the humanities. More recently, there has been concern about the fact that girls settle to learning more easily than boys and are gradually overtaking them in many spheres.

Teachers reinforce some children more effectively than others. Kelly (1989), for example, in a study which reviews research into gender differences, notes that there was considerable evidence that girls received less of the teacher's attention in class than boys. This was true for all ages, ethnic groups and social classes in all subjects and with both male and female teachers.

In a study in Clwyd (1983) there was evidence in science lessons that in mixed groups boys tended to carry out the practical work, leaving the girls to clear up and write up the experiment. Boys were in the front places for demonstrations and fewer girls asked questions.

A study by Graham (1994), describing GCSE results and evidence leading up to them in four schools in Hampshire, found measurable differences between boys' and girls' responses to school. Girls gained better results than boys and showed greater satisfaction with school, greater commitment and a more positive attitude to teachers all the way through the school. When asked to account for this, the students suggested that baby boys are more desired and treasured than baby girls and grow to expect a larger slice of the cake!

Martinson (1994) describes a project in Humberside involving a secondary school and five primary schools, which concluded that boys needed help to achieve more in English and languages. She quotes the evidence from 51 inspection reports that girls consistently out-performed boys in English. There were few schools that monitored these differences and none with special programmes to improve boys' performance.

A study by Sadker and Sadker described by Wilce (1985) showed teachers reinforcing boys more than girls in their responses. Boys were about eight times more likely than girls to call out in class. These findings were consistent in all types of classes and teachers were unaware that this was happening. After training, teachers treated their students equally and girls began to take a more active part in lessons.

Race

A group of Ealing teachers working together in 1974 stated a number of aims for multiracial education, which are still valid. Four of them were concerned with affective education. All pupils should:

- have confidence in their sense of their own identities;
- accept strangeness without fear or threat;
- respect the uniqueness of each individual;
- respect the achievement of cultures different from their own.

There is a sense in which we all are prejudiced in favour of our own culture. We need to work at taking a wider view. Our students are growing up in a world in which they need to accept a wide range of people and cultures. Some schools are able to offer students the opportunity to get to know people of different races, because they have mixed populations. Others need to make an effort to do this. Many schools try to provide opportunities for their students to travel abroad, sometimes to Third World countries, and this is very valuable, although some young people will be unable to afford these trips.

It is very easy for a teacher, without being aware of it, to stereotype students of different races and to have different expectations of them. It is easy to do this with any student, but where a boy or girl has a black skin it is even easier for white teachers. The expectations help to create self-fulfilling prophecies. It is necessary to work to see students as individuals.

It is also necessary for the teacher to learn something of the body language of other cultures. West Indian children, for example, tend not to make eye contact out of deference to the teacher. This tends to be misunderstood by teachers. It is a task for all teachers to monitor their behaviour towards ethnic minority students, so that they are not expecting too little from them or expecting only certain kinds of behaviour.

Many students from ethnic minorities have the problem that English is not their first language and is not usually spoken in the home. Even where it is, it may be a different variety of English, which can interfere with the use of standard English required in school.

Social background

Working-class students tend to be stereotyped and attract comparatively low expectations, especially if their speech is strongly regional. They tend to have lower self-esteem than those from more privileged backgrounds. Many working-class students are part of a cycle of poor achievement. Their parents did not do well at school and wrote off education as something that was not of much value, passing on this view to their children. The school may have to convince parents as well as students that achievement is possible and important in a world where unskilled jobs are fast disappearing.

Working-class students have the disadvantage that many of the values of the school, such as the importance of deferring satisfaction, academic success and non-violence, may conflict with the values of home. They may also have the disadvantage that the use of language at home differs from that in school, although by the time they enter the secondary school they should have acquired a good deal of standard English.

Hargreaves (1982: 17) suggests that school destroys the dignity of many working-class children. He describes this as follows: 'To have dignity means to have a sense of being worthy of possessing creative, inventive and critical capacities, of having power to achieve personal and social change. When dignity is damaged, one's deepest experience is of being inferior, unable and powerless.'

Low ability and disability

The poor performance of the least able in our schools has been a matter for concern for a long time. Other countries succeed with a much wider proportion of the population, and countries such as Japan take the view that anyone can achieve if he or she is prepared to work. The coming of the National Curriculum has placed new demands on schools and we can no longer offer young people who appear to be lacking in ability a limited curriculum, except in particular circumstances.

Low-ability students now have to follow the National Curriculum. This places considerable demands on them and on their teachers. The school has a responsibility to see that they have as many opportunities as more able students, because it is through new experiences that they may move forward.

It is easy to underestimate students with disabilities, particularly where these involve speech problems or physical problems. Many disabled people are able to achieve a surprising amount when given the opportunity and the desire to achieve, and physical disability does not necessarily mean mental disability. It can be revealing to visit a special school and look at what is achieved with students of low ability.

Hargreaves (1982: 62) suggests that if less able students 'understand that they lack the very quality by which the school sets most store, a sense of failure tends to permeate the whole personality leaving a feeling of powerlessness and hopelessness.'

CONTINUITY

The child and young person needs to engage in education from nursery school to school leaving and beyond as one continuous experience. Discontinuity slows progress and wastes the time of both students and teacher. If students spend the first year of the secondary school repeating what they have done in the last year of the primary school this damages their motivation and they lose interest.

Students will now move through the National Curriculum at different speeds, and it will be necessary for the secondary school to know and carry on from the point each child has reached in the primary school. Primary schools are now obliged to give a report on the stage each child transferring has reached. This means that secondary school teachers need to plan work at a variety of levels.

Ideally there should be intervisiting between primary and secondary schools, so that each comes to understand how the other works, although this can be difficult when a secondary school serves many primary schools and only a few students come from each.

The more that secondary school teachers know about the work of the primary school, the better they are able to help new students to adapt to the much larger world of the secondary school. When children enter the secondary school they are usually very worried about doing things that will get them into trouble, yet they can easily find themselves behaving in ways that would have been acceptable in their primary school, but that are no longer acceptable in the secondary school. For example, in most primary schools, children go and get whatever they need for their work without asking permission. This may not be the case in some secondary classes, and this needs to be explained. There are many unwritten rules of this kind, and intake year teachers need to give some thought to how students should be expected to get to know them. Discussion between primary and secondary teachers about expectations in terms of behaviour and social maturity can be useful here. Primary schools tend to expect a good deal more from their year 6 children than secondary schools expect from them in year 7.

Most secondary schools now arrange visits to the secondary school by primary children, who are often shown round by older students and undertake some interesting work. Some also arrange visits to primary schools by secondary students to talk about their experience and answer questions.

The move from primary to secondary school is not the only point at which there is the possibility of discontinuity. There can be discontinuity between years, especially if there is a change of teacher in any subject. In particular, there can be discontinuity between years 9 and 10 and between the main school and the sixth form. If some subjects are not to be continued, it is important that the courses experienced in the first three years are seen as self-contained and constitute complete courses in their own right.

The break between the main school and the sixth form is substantial for some students. They need to have been gradually increasing the extent to which they are expected to work independently if they are to cope with the demands of sixth form study.

The last break is that of leaving school for work or for further or higher education. Schools are now preparing young people much more thoroughly for the world of work than in the past. The ability to settle happily into further or higher education depends, on the one hand, on the degree of independence in learning a young person has achieved and, on the other, on the social maturity and ability to live and work with others which has been developed in school.

Continuity concerns not only students but also their parents. Parents need to be introduced to the ways of the secondary school and the expectations the school has for the partnership of school and parents.

The National Curriculum makes it easier for teachers to see the curriculum in continuity from the start of schooling to the end of the compulsory period. Teachers at the secondary school stage need to be familiar with the stages that have gone before, and the way in which the child's skill and knowledge have been built up, because they need to take students on from the point in the National Curriculum that they have reached.

Continuity is related to progression and development. Progression may be evident in the work of the individual students, and it is valuable for the staff of a department to discuss what is meant by progression in their subject. This is not an easy task, partly because in the past we have tended to think of content in terms of knowledge to be acquired, rather than as skills and concepts. The National Curriculum is largely stated in terms of skills and concepts, but it is still necessary to consider what may be considered progression in any given area. Students do not acquire concepts in one go. They take steps towards acquiring them and consideration of those steps can be extremely helpful in dealing with the slower learners. It can be salutary to see the way in which special school teachers break down statements of attainment into much smaller steps to enable slower students to work towards the final statement.

Development is concerned with the way in which increasing maturity enables students to undertake tasks requiring more abstract knowledge. In physical education and subjects requiring strength and dexterity, the physical development of students will also be important.

If there is to be continuity between primary and secondary schools, an effort should be made to dispel the myths that teachers at each stage hold about each other, and to enable each sector to understand the teaching approaches which are common at the previous or the succeeding stage. This means that teachers should visit each other and observe teaching. This will not be easy to arrange, but with determination it can be done. It is also useful to provide opportunities for primary and secondary teachers to discuss teaching methods as seen by teachers and to ask students about how they see teaching methods in their primary and secondary schools as differing.

Checklist 3 – The students

- How many of the students in my classes do I know by name?
- What am I doing which enhances the self-image of the students I teach?
- What do I do which conveys that I have high but realistic expectations for all students?
- Do I underestimate any group of students?
- Do I provide for the range of ability in my classes?
- Do I give sufficient thought to the language I use with my classes?
- Do the students in my classes have the opportunity to learn through discussion?
- Do I do enough to find out what ideas the students have before starting on a new topic?
- What forms of motivation do I use?
- Do I treat any group of students differently? If I do, can I justify this?
- What do I know about the primary schools from which students in the intake year come?
- What values am I helping my students to acquire?

CONCLUSION

Today's young people are growing up in difficult circumstances. Crime has been on the increase and a number are tempted into criminal activities. Drugs are fairly easily available and young people may be tempted to try soft drugs and eventually move on to hard drugs. They then need to find money for their addiction. There is peer group pressure to own certain things and dress in certain ways, all of which cost money, which parents may not be able to supply. Unemployment in many parts of the country has taken away some of the incentive to do well at school and obtain qualifications. Many boys and girls are the product of broken homes or single-parent families and some may have considerable responsibilities at home. Both boys and girls may have to cope with the emotional effects of family break-up. For some, school may be the only stable part of their lives.

There is now a good deal of research evidence to show that school makes a difference (e.g. Rutter *et al.* 1979; Mortimore *et al.* 1988). Schools with similar backgrounds and populations differ in their success academically and in social education. The good school not only gives students a good academic education but also helps them to develop a framework of values which enables them to solve moral problems and deal with the many problems that are part of living in our society.

FURTHER READING

Cohen, L. and Manion, L. (1989) *A Guide to Teaching Practice,* 3rd edn. London: Routledge. Contains a useful section on learning.

Davis, L. (1985) *Caring for Secondary School Pupils.* London: Heinemann. An account of a study of secondary school students which gives many insights into the way adolescents think and behave.

Hamblin, D. (1974) *The Teacher and Counselling.* Oxford: Blackwell. This book is written for teachers who have a major counselling role but, though old now, it has a great deal to say about counselling that would be of value to any teacher.

Kyriacou, C. (1986) *Effective Teaching in Schools.* Oxford: Blackwell. Deals with research on learning and looks at effective learning as well as effective teaching.

Sutton, C. (ed.) (1981) *Communicating in the Classroom.* London: Hodder and Stoughton. Looks at talking and writing as forms of communication and learning in the classroom.

4

THE TEACHER

THE ROLE OF THE SECONDARY SCHOOL TEACHER

Teachers are professional people. Being professional means having a theoretical background to the work you do and having a professional code of behaviour. Capel *et al.* (1995: 20) make the following points about this:

> There is a professional code of ethics which is currently unwritten in the UK but which you are expected to uphold. For example, you are expected to treat information about individuals with confidentiality; provide equal opportunities for the pupils in your care; deal with pupils in an objective, professional manner regardless of your personal feelings; keep up to date in your subject; reflect on and develop your teaching; adopt appropriate language and a professional demeanour.

Teachers in the secondary school have in many ways a more difficult task than their primary colleagues, in that they see numbers of different groups of students in the course of each day. This makes it more difficult to get to know students well, especially for those teachers who see very large numbers in the course of a week. The task is made even more difficult by the fact that the students are at a stage when they are likely to challenge teachers in many ways.

The teacher's role in the secondary school involves not only classroom teaching of a subject or subjects but also very often a role as a tutor with pastoral care responsibilities for a group of students. There may be other roles in extra-curricular activities, in helping students to produce plays and concerts, for example, or in games and clubs of various kinds.

THE TEACHER'S COMPETENCIES

In 1992 the Department for Education issued a circular which listed the competencies it felt should be part of initial teacher training (see Appendix). Since then the Teacher Training Agency (1994) has updated this list in relation to newly qualified teachers as part of proposals for developing profiles for teachers at the end of their training. Their list, which is being revised, is as follows.

Knowledge and understanding of the Curriculum

NQTs (newly qualified teachers) should have knowledge and understanding of the school curriculum for the age phase for which they have been trained, and should be able to ensure continuity and progression within their own class and with the classes to and from which their pupils transfer.

In the secondary phase, NQTs should be able to demonstrate an understanding

- of the place of their subject(s) in the school curriculum;
- of the framework of the statutory requirements.

They should be able to:

- contribute to the development of pupils' language and communication skills.

Subject knowledge and subject application

In the secondary phase, competences in this area should be demonstrated in

- knowledge and understanding of the National Curriculum;
- a breadth and depth of subject knowledge extending beyond programmes of study and examination syllabuses;
- the ability to plan coherent lessons, teach and assess, taking account of National Curriculum requirements and school curriculum policies.

Teaching strategies and classroom management

NQTs should be able to:

- identify and respond to relevant individual differences between pupils and to set appropriately demanding expectations for learning performance;
- employ a range of teaching strategies appropriate to the age, ability and attainment of pupils, and decide when teaching the whole class, groups or individuals is appropriate for particular learning purposes;
- present subject content and learning tasks in a clear and stimulating manner so as to maintain pupils' interest and motivation;
- communicate clearly and effectively with pupils through questioning, instructing, explaining and feedback;

- make constructive use of information technology and other resources for learning;
- create and maintain a purposeful, orderly and supportive environment for their pupils' learning by establishing clear expectations of behaviour in the classroom, setting appropriate standards of discipline and using suitable rewards and sanctions.

Assessment and recording of pupils' progress

NQTs should be able to:

- judge how well each pupil performs against appropriate criteria and standards, by identifying individual pupils' attainment with reference to relevant National Curriculum requirements;
- assess and record systematically the progress of individual pupils;
- use such assessment in their planning and teaching;
- provide oral and written feedback to pupils on their progress;
- prepare and present reports on pupils' progress to colleagues and parents.

Foundation for further professional development

NQTs should have acquired in initial teacher training the necessary foundation to develop:

- a working knowledge of their contractual, legal, administrative and pastoral responsibilities as teachers;
- effective working relationships with colleagues and parents;
- vision, imagination and critical awareness in educating their pupils;
- the ability to recognize diversity of talent, including that of gifted pupils, and to identify special educational needs or learning difficulties;
- a self-critical approach to diagnosing and evaluating pupils' learning and the ability to recognize the effect on that learning of teachers' expectations and actions;
- a readiness to promote the spiritual, moral, social and cultural development of pupils.

WHAT THE TEACHER NEEDS TO KNOW

Teachers in secondary schools need a considerable amount of knowledge in addition to their subject knowledge. They will also be learning from doing the work and a good teacher goes on learning throughout teaching life. The school in which you start your teaching career plays an important part in your professional development even if it is not a very good school. You can learn from negative examples as well as positive ones.

Bennett and Carré (1993: 7) suggest that there are a number of knowledge bases needed by teachers:

- content knowledge;
- general pedagogical knowledge;
- curriculum knowledge;
- pedagogical content knowledge;
- knowledge of learners and their characteristics;
- knowledge of educational ends, purposes and values, and philosophical and historical grounds.

This was written with primary school teachers in mind but is nevertheless relevant to secondary school teachers. It can be more specifically adapted for secondary school teachers. The following sub-sections detail what is needed by the teacher.

Self-knowledge

You need to know your strengths and weaknesses as a teacher so that you can build on the strengths and work to develop the weaknesses. Your students react to the way that you behave and when you are not happy with the result it is worth looking at what you did as well as what the students did.

A thought out philosophy

Good teachers have a clear idea of what the educational process is about, and have broad aims which underlie the work they do. Your values and ideas about education give you a yardstick by which you can assess your performance and also by which to assess new ideas. However, your views about the educational process should develop and clarify as you go on teaching. Most teachers start with an ideal of what they would like to do and gradually modify their views in the light of experience. The important thing is to maintain an ideal and not become cynical. It is also important to reflect on your practice, looking at whether it matches up to your values.

Adolescent development

There is a brief account of this in Chapter 3. Your training will also have dealt with this, and your memory of your own development and your observation of young people in school will add to this knowledge, so that you gradually develop an understanding of a wide range of young people and a sympathy with them, which enables you to work with them and stimulate their learning.

How people learn

The following points should be borne in mind.

Learning depends upon motivation (this was discussed in Chapter 3). The human power to learn is considerable, and in most schools we succeed in tapping only a small amount of this power. If you think of the complexity of learning language which is acquired before schooling starts by virtually all young children, you realize that there is much more power for learning present than you often see in school. Young people also often show great power for learning in their use of computers. Most people are motivated by problems that are challenging but within their capacity, and not enough education is seen in these terms. Your task is to find the motivation that taps into this power for learning.

Learning is an active process. Students have to make learning their own by using it or talking about it. Material needs to be absorbed to the level of use. Merely being able to repeat what has been learned is not enough.

Learning needs to be made accessible and usable. We remember things when they make a pattern (see pp. 60–2). This means that learning needs to be structured in students' minds. Structuring involves matching it to what the learners know already and helping them to classify the knowledge into categories so that it is easy to recall. Students need to learn to structure learning for themselves as well as having it structured for them.

Language means only as much as the experience it represents. Students learn from the words of others when they can match the words with their own experience. It is easy to assume that younger and less able students have experience and should understand what is being said when this is not the case. Sotto (1994: 56) expresses this as follows: 'We often think we have conveyed the meaning of something when we have said something. But we only manage to convey meaning when the person to whom we are speaking already has that meaning.' As learners all have different experiences they will all process new knowledge differently. It is therefore important that what is learned is discussed, so that learners have a chance to modify their views in the light of what others have to say.

Reward and praise are more effective than blame and punishment. This has been demonstrated by research, but the knowledge tends to be used in a very limited way. It is possible to guide learning by rewarding very specific behaviour, particularly where students pose problems (see Chapter 6).

Sotto (1994: 110) suggests that if people's natural capacity to learn has not been impaired, it looks as if they learn best when:

- they find that there is something which they wish to learn;
- they are able to tackle this task reasonably directly;
- the task offers intrinsic rewards;
- the task is sensible and manageable;
- they can formulate hunches, test them and see the result of their action;
- they are able to see patterns;
- they find themselves in a challenging but friendly and supportive environment.

If the teacher is too critical this tends to inhibit learning. Sotto (1994) found that even when criticism was constructive people became defensive. He

Checklist 4 – The teacher's knowledge

Self-knowledge

- What are my strengths?
- What are my weaknesses?

Philosophy

- What do I believe is really important in education at the secondary stage?
- What are my priorities?
- What are the implications of what I believe for what I do in school?

Adolescent development

- Do I know enough about the normal patterns of development to recognize deviations from them?
- Do I take development into account sufficiently when I plan work?

Student learning

- What motivation do I use to encourage student learning?
- Are my students sufficiently active in their learning?
- Is what they are learning accessible and usable?
- Do I help students to structure what they are learning?
- Do I take enough account of the need to match language to student experience?
- Do I praise students enough?

Group behaviour

- Am I satisfied with the overall behaviour in my classes?
- How often do I praise good behaviour and how often do I comment on bad behaviour?
- Do I praise or reprove the same students every time?
- What am I doing to teach my students to work cooperatively?
- Have I a good balance between cooperation and competition?

Subject matter

- Do I do enough to find out what students already know about new topics?
- Am I helping students to structure their learning?
- Am I doing enough to train students to become independent learners?
- How well are students retaining what they learn?

suggests that this problem can be overcome by concentrating on how work can be improved.

Group behaviour

Teaching in school depends upon the teacher's ability to manage students in groups. In the first place you need to be able to manage the class as a group. You may then break it up into smaller groups for some purposes but you still need to be able to manage this situation. Some subjects, such as dance, drama and games, depend upon working in groups.

Group behaviour varies according to the composition of the group and, in the secondary school, each group you teach will have its own ethos, depending upon its composition. Certain students within the group will serve as models and leaders of others, and may set the standards in positive or negative ways. Young people not only use other students as models but are themselves controlled by the group.

You can sometimes use the desire to be part of the group to get conforming behaviour, which is an essential prerequisite for school learning. By picking out a particular student for praise or blame you indicate to the group what you want.

The class may be supportive to all its members or to only some of them. It may be cooperative, both in working and in avoiding work, or competitive, with certain individuals trying to outdo others.

What works well with one group will not necessarily work well with another. Classes have their own personalities, which you need to take into account when planning work. Group work is discussed in Chapter 5.

Subject matter

Secondary schools have the advantage that most of their teachers are specialists in their subject areas, although staff cuts may mean that some people are teaching subjects in which they are not specialists. To be a good teacher in a secondary school you need to be expert in your particular area, so that you can select from a wide store of knowledge the best material to teach the National Curriculum to each of your classes. In addition, as we have already seen, you need to train your students so that they gradually become independent learners in your specialist area.

You also need to go on learning in your specialism, since no subject stands still. New research is continually turning up new information, and you need to do all you can to keep up with this.

TEACHING SKILLS

You also need to know a number of ways of presenting knowledge and teaching skills and concepts. If every lesson follows a similar pattern, students will soon become bored and difficult. You need the following skills.

Observing and interpreting student behaviour

This is a basic skill of teaching. The only way you have of knowing what students can do and understand is what you can observe by way of behaviour or as a result of questioning them or looking at their work. You need to be able to read student body language so that you are able to anticipate trouble, identify those who need help, know the signs of under-functioning and recognize the stage of development and understanding of some students. It takes time to learn how to do this, but all teachers come into teaching with considerable skill in reading the non-verbal signals that others send out, because this is part of human behaviour. You have to learn to apply this knowledge in the classroom. Body language is dealt with in more detail in Chapter 6.

In addition to general observation, it may be helpful from time to time to make a particular point of observing systematically the behaviour of a small number of students in each class, particularly those who pose problems. In doing this you may see how such students create problems and learn to recognize the point at which you might intervene.

Observation includes looking at the work of individuals and drawing conclusions from it, particularly at the beginning of the year or with a new class when you want to know how much they already know and understand. You also need to observe to assess the effect of your teaching. It can be helpful, if you feel confident enough to do it, to ask your students for views about particular pieces of work.

Organization and control

You will not be able to teach successfully unless you have developed these skills. They are skills that look easy in the hands of an experienced and competent teacher but take time to learn. Control of a class is partly dependent on confidence, and this needs to develop over time, but inexperienced teachers can learn the body language and tone of voice that demonstrate confidence. It is also a question of recognizing challenges to your authority as teacher and dealing with them before they escalate. This is dealt with in more detail in Chapter 6.

Control requires you to set clear rules for classroom behaviour at the very beginning of work with a new group, and to insist on conformity. You may involve the students in developing the rules, and it is important to explain the purpose of the rules to them so that they can see the reasons for them. This is described in further detail in Chapter 6.

Control in the classroom is most difficult at points of change. There may be problems at the beginning of a lesson as students come in, problems as you change activity and problems in clearing up at the end. You can anticipate these problems by very careful and well thought out instructions.

Communication

The ability to form good relationships with students is an essential prerequisite of good teaching. Unless you can relate well to students and they to you, you will not teach successfully. Forming good relationships means that you communicate that you like young people, that you respect them individually, that you care about them and believe that they can do well. Most of this is communicated informally in the way you deal with individuals and with groups. While it is not really possible to treat younger secondary school students as adults, it is sometimes salutary to compare your treatment of your students with the way you would treat another adult. Do you give them a comparable amount of respect as individuals?

There is a sense in which the teacher's role is similar to that of an actor, and his or her activity in front of a class is a performance. This does not mean that you are being other than yourself, but that an audience the size of a class needs very clear messages, in terms of what is said, how it is said and body language. When speaking to the whole class, good teachers emphasize their message by their tone of voice and use gestures that tend to be larger than those they use in the staffroom because of the need to get a message to a large group. Good speakers speaking to adults do much the same thing.

Skill in communication is an essential part of teaching. Communication takes place as a result of people attending to each other. The way you convey your message determines how far students attend to you. Your voice and the way you move should encourage attention. Your view of your listeners is demonstrated in your choice of content, vocabulary and sentence structure, and in the variation you make in pitch and pace and the use of pauses. If the response you get is not what you hoped for, you will give your message again in a slightly different and simpler form, almost without thinking about it.

Movement is the most basic form of communication, operating from birth or perhaps even earlier. Because it is so basic, its message goes over even when you actually say something different. Movement and gesture are continuously sending messages to others. Your observation of your students involves interpreting the movement messages they send, and their observation of you plays a similar part. Neill and Caswell (1993: xvi) make this point very tellingly:

Non-verbal signals are more powerful in conveying feelings than speech because most recipients are unaware of them. If you overtly tell a class that the subject you are dealing with is really exciting or that you intend to deal firmly with any indiscipline, the explicit message may give the more cynical members of the class a clear target to aim for. If you convey enthusiasm or firmness non-verbally, your audience extracts the message from your behaviour subliminally. Since they have derived the message themselves without being aware of having done so, they are less likely to be able to challenge it.

Eye contact is an important aspect of communication. By making eye contact with individual students you make them aware that they are being noticed and had better behave or that they are important and are being cared for.

There are three specific areas of communication which are essential to teaching.

Presentation includes narrative, describing and explaining. Wragg and Brown (1993: 3) describe explaining as 'giving understanding to another'. Most studies of what students want from their teachers place the ability to explain well at the top of the list.

Explaining and presenting material to classes requires careful preparation. Your opening should give a general idea of what you want to talk about. You then give your presentation and conclude by going over the main points of what you have said. In preparing you need to consider the key ideas in what you want to get over and the logical order in which you need to put the material across. Language, both vocabulary and structure, needs to be appropriate for the group for which you are preparing. You may also need to think about what aids you may need and how you intend to use them. This is dealt with in more detail in Chapter 5.

Questioning may be part of the explanation process, and this too needs preparation. Kerry (1980) states that the primary purpose of questioning is to encourage students' talk. You need to encourage students to talk about what they know already about a topic you are about to introduce. You also need them to talk about what they have understood from your explanations or other learning opportunities, such as videos or field work.

There are many ways of describing the kind of questions that can be asked. A major division is between closed questions, which have a specific answer, and open questions, which require students to speculate and think ahead. Brown and Wragg (1993) note the tendency of teachers to ask mainly factual questions, with a comparatively small number of higher order questions that require thought. They note that the teachers who taught the most stimulating lessons asked questions which involved students in looking ahead and their key questions related to the expressed aims of their lessons. Questioning is dealt with in greater detail in Chapter 5.

Discussion. Students need to talk about what they have learned and are learning if they are to make it their own. You can arrange for whole-class discussion or give them the opportunity to discuss in pairs or small groups. Either way, you need to be very clear about what is to be discussed. Small discussion groups need a brief that they can understand and use as a guide for discussion, and you also need your own brief for whole-class discussion.

Whole-class discussion is not as easy as it looks in the hands of an expert teacher. If it really takes off you may have more people wanting to speak than there is time for. On the other hand, you may have difficulty getting people to contribute at all. If this is the case, you need to look carefully at how you are dealing with the contributions students make. You may not be welcoming enough to what individuals say, so that others are not prepared to risk saying anything. It is also sometimes difficult with a new class to get discussion going, because they are testing out how you will react to what they say and are not prepared to risk too much at an early stage. It can often be better to start with some discussion in pairs and then have a class discussion of the same topic. This will give students the opportunity to think out what they want to say, and they will therefore find it easier to contribute to general discussion. You also need to scan the group constantly to see who wants to speak.

If your students are really to gain from whole-class discussion, you need to sum up what is being said from time to time and relate it to the work you have done or are planning to do, and in particular you need to sum up at the end of the discussion. There is further information about discussion in Chapter 5.

Planning

Every teacher needs to be a good planner. You need to make plans for the year, for the term and for the next week and the next day. Each piece of work you do needs to fit into an overall pattern that is more detailed than the National Curriculum. If you are a form tutor you will also need to make plans for your work in any tutorial periods with your form. Planning is dealt with in more detail in Chapter 2.

Decision-making

A teacher is continually making decisions. As you become more experienced you are able to draw on past experience as well as your value system to decide how to deal with a particular situation, but new teachers have to make decisions about situations by drawing only on their value system and what they have learned in training.

Bishop and Whitfield (1972: 4) suggest that a good or effective teacher is:

- Aware of the variables which can be under his [*sic*] control.
- Aware of the likely effects of manipulating these variables in different ways.
- Able to manipulate them so that he [*sic*] can achieve what he [*sic*] regards as effective learning by the pupils in his [*sic*] care.

The variables under the teacher's control are the choice of teaching strategies, the organization of pupils for learning, the language used, the sequencing of learning material and the materials chosen. The teacher not only has to make decisions about each of these in planning but also has to make decisions moment by moment in the classroom in response to the way students appear to be learning and behaving. This involves decisions about the implementation of what has been planned, the language and gestures used, the examples given, the way students' responses are dealt with, motivation of students and discipline and social control.

To each decision you bring your own idea of what is important in dealing with students and ideas of what is important in the subject matter being taught. As you build up experience, this will affect the way you make decisions, because you will be able to draw on past experience of similar situations in many cases. You will also have made judgements about whether the way you dealt with a situation was effective and will have tried to repeat effective decisions and avoid those that were unsuccessful.

There are decisions that you need to make outside the classroom. Some of these are to do with your role as form tutor and others with your membership of a department and other groups. Your role in social control and discipline is also present outside the classroom and around the school.

Problem-solving

Teaching is a problem-solving activity. You are constantly looking at the best way to put over the material you want to teach, dealing with students who pose specific problems, managing with the resources available to you and so on. Students also need to become problem-solvers. Work in technology supports this, but there is a sense in which problem-solving can come into every area of the curriculum, and it is also part of the learning process, since students have to solve the problems of how to set about learning something, how to fit in homework and other interests and much else.

A useful way to consider problems is first to define the problem in some detail and consider where you want to get to. For example, you may be concerned about the wide range of ability in some of your classes and want to get to the stage where you are providing for the full range. The next stage is to think about all the possible solutions.

Force field analysis, devised by Lewin (1947), is one useful method of looking at problems. It involves looking at the forces which are in your favour and those which are working against you in dealing with a problem. Let us suppose that in this case the forces in your favour are that your department has a wide range of materials for different ability groups, and your head of department is both supportive and skilled in dealing with mixed-ability groups. Against you is the fact that the groups tend to be on the large side, the range of ability is really very wide and you feel pressed for time. This suggests that you first consult with your head of department for ideas about how to tackle your problem.

There are really two main approaches to dealing with a class with a wide range of ability. You can give different groups different work leading to the same end, but with some tasks given in simpler language and some demanding extra. You have access to a range of materials and may be able to find suitable material to match the abilities of different groups of students.

Another possibility is to set more open-ended work which can be dealt with at different levels. For example, in history or geography the question 'How would our lives be different if we lived in a different (specified) environment with a different climate or at a different (specified) time in history?' could be discussed by mixed ability groups before the information is summarized at a whole-class level. Students of all abilities should have some ideas about this, and the more able should be able to take it much further with more ideas. In questioning, more open-ended questions will give the more able a chance, while still making it possible for the less able to answer.

A further point is to spend some time on study skills. Helping students to read intelligently and sort out how they are going to set down their ideas may mean that a number can work more independently. Another approach would be to try paired tutoring, with students teaching each other. This is described in more detail in Chapter 5.

Jackson (1975) suggests that one should consider the obstacles in the way of solving a problem and consider whether one could overcome an obstacle, go round it, remove it, demolish it, neutralize it, prove it to be illusory, turn it to advantage, buy it off, alter it, find its weakest point or wait for it to go away. When one addresses oneself directly to an obstacle there are frequently ways forward. A useful strategy is to ask a series of questions such as: can I overcome the problem by looking at it a different way, by using materials differently, by looking for time to do some basic thinking and sorting out ideas in order to move forward, by working with colleagues, by involving parents or others, by getting students to work differently, by reorganizing the situation or the use of materials and so on? This kind of thinking is often most profitably undertaken in a group.

It is also sometimes a useful activity for students as well as interested staff. Galton (1989) describes a discussion with older primary school children, where the teacher posed them the problem that she was unable to deal adequately with them as individuals, because so many kept coming to her for minor kinds of help. After discussion the class decided to keep a record of when they went to the teacher and as a result of this concluded that they could help each other a great deal more.

Evaluation

Evaluation is dealt with in detail in Chapter 10, but it can be noted here that you need the ability to evaluate the work of the students formatively and summatively and to evaluate your own work as well. It takes time to build up your knowledge of what it is reasonable to expect at each stage in the secondary school and it is a good idea while you are building up this skill to talk to other teachers of your subject about this and to ask them to show you work that they consider to be good at each stage.

TEACHING STYLE

Every teacher develops his or her own style or way of doing things. At first you draw on the models of teachers you experienced as a student as well as those you have seen during your training, but gradually you start to build a

Checklist 5 – The teacher's skills

Observation

- How good were the assessments I made of my new classes when they first came to me?
- Do my records give me the information I need to provide appropriately for my students?
- Am I aware of the needs of the most and least able in my classes?
- Am I making sufficient observation of the effect of my teaching?

Organization and control

- Am I satisfied with my control of my classes? Is there anything I need to improve?
- Can I always get attention when I wish?
- Have I set clear rules for classroom behaviour?
- Am I able to enforce them?
- Am I providing a sufficient variety of organizational patterns to keep students interested?
- Am I happy with what happens at the beginning and end of lessons and when we change the organization?
- Am I providing adequately for the most and least able students?

Communication

- How well do I present material to the whole class?
- Do I explain things clearly?
- Does my questioning include enough higher order questions?
- Am I able to lead a class discussion adequately? Do students respond well?
- Do I involve all members of the class equally in asking for responses?
- Do I always respond positively to students' answers?

Planning

- Do I start planning with aims and objectives?
- Do I plan long term as well as short term?
- Do my plans take into consideration the composition of my classes?
- Do my plans include the teaching of appropriate study skills?
- Do I set dates for finishing parts of my plans?
- Do I make plans for evaluating my work?
- Do I plan to meet my development needs in relation to particular work?

Decision-making
- By what criteria do I make decisions about: subject matter for teaching; teaching strategies; discipline and control?
- Do I evaluate enough of my decisions?

Problem-solving
- Do I treat problems as something to be solved by logical processes?
- Do I identify clearly specific problems in my work?
- Do I work at solving problems?

Evaluation
- Am I building up my knowledge of what constitutes good work at each stage?
- Am I evaluating my own work sufficiently?
- Am I evaluating adequately the work of each group I teach?

style of your own. Most teachers, particularly the inexperienced, have only a limited number of styles on which to model themselves. It is therefore wise to take every opportunity you can to see other people teach. In the course of doing this you will see ways of doing things which seem to fit for you.

Influences on style

In the first instance, style is a matter of personality. It depends upon the kind of person you are. Your training and your experience of watching other teachers at work also affect your style by giving you a choice of ways of working, and those you choose gradually become part of your personal style. You also become more confident and sure of yourself as you go on teaching and your style becomes more individual and personal.

Your style, like your decision-making, will also be influenced by what you think important in teaching, by your overall philosophy of education and your values. All teachers hold views that affect the way they work, without necessarily recognizing them as a philosophy. These may change as you become more experienced.

Finally, your teaching style is affected by the particular context in which you are working, and in particular by the first school in which you work as a teacher, which is usually very influential in that it is experience that comes when you are building up your style. The particular groups of students you teach demand different approaches and you will work differently with year 7 and with the sixth form. You will also work differently in an inner-city school compared with a school in a prosperous suburb or a country school. You may have to learn that a somewhat different style is demanded when you move to a different school.

Demonstrating style

Style shows in the way you work. It is evident in what you decide to do as a teacher, in the way you present material, your questioning style, your use of time in the classroom, the way you organize work and the teaching strategies you use. It will also be evident in the way you deal with students, both in helping them in their work and in controlling them and managing the discipline of the classroom. The way you communicate with students is all part of your style. Some teachers tend to talk down to students and others talk at a level which is stimulating, so that students have to think hard to follow what is being said. There is also a difference in the amount teachers talk and in the amount of time they give to encouraging students to talk. Cohen and Manion (1983: 226) make the point that humour is valuable: 'it relaxes tension, helps establish natural relationships, facilitates learning and is of great value as a means of restoring sanity to a classroom after a disciplinary incident.'

Students match their learning style to the teacher's style, so that they will work differently for different teachers.

STUDENTS' VIEWS OF WHAT THEY WANT FROM TEACHERS

Children's views of their teachers change as they grow older. Fontana (1985: 9) suggests that secondary school students look for expertise, especially 'the kind of competence that indicates success in what they see as desirable areas in adult life.' They become more critical of adults as they move through the secondary school and are more likely to blame adults for their own failures and question and challenge authority.

Wragg (1984: 82) undertook a study of the opinions of 200 pupils, 50 from each of four year groups, equally divided between boys and girls. Pupils were asked 'to imagine the best teacher in the world' and then say whether a number of statements would apply. Eighty-four per cent said that this teacher would introduce himself by name and would give some information about himself. The statements which showed strongest agreement suggested that the teacher would explain things clearly, would call students by their first name, would help the slower ones catch up in a nice way, would help students to learn a lot in every lesson and would be a good listener.

Wragg followed up this survey by interviewing 25 students in groups of two or three. This led to a description of one teacher rated highly by students. He spent time on rules of behaviour and invited students to add to them on occasion. He then enforced them. He was rated highly on confidence, being businesslike and warm. He maintained high eye contact with individual students and had a quick reaction to the first signs of misdemeanour. He showed a ready humour, used surprise and was interested in the students' work, especially after they had been reprimanded.

Wragg concluded that 'The pupils in this sample liked teachers who were firm but fair, consistent, stimulating, interested in individuals and had a sense of humour and they disliked those who showed the polar opposites of these characteristics' (p. 95). This is confirmed by Denscombe (1985: 97–8), who states that pupils expect teachers to:

- Be firm. First and foremost the 'good' teacher is willing and able to exercise control over individuals and classes. But the methods used to achieve this control also serve to separate the good from the bad.
- Be fair. The good teacher does not give punishments that are seen as too harsh and is careful to give punishments only to 'guilty parties'. He/she also avoids the use of adverse comparisons between individuals or groups of pupils as a means of achieving control.
- Be respectful to pupils. The good teacher allows pupils to retain a sense of dignity which is especially valued by adolescent pupils.
- Be friendly. The good teacher is not aloof or distant. He/she must be able to 'have a laugh' and be able to 'take a joke'.
- Explain things well and get work done. The good teacher establishes productive lessons and avoids boring lessons, so that pupils feel they have achieved something and are interested in the subject.

It should be remembered that the teacher can be a model for the students. Cohen and Manion (1989: 264–5) state that 'A warm and enthusiastic teacher whom the children like will be imitated by them.' They go on to say: 'Good teachers model respect for others by treating children politely and pleasantly and by avoiding behaviour which would cause them to suffer indignities.'

FURTHER READING

Brown, G. and Wragg, E.C. (1993) *Questioning.* London: Routledge. Wragg, E.C. and Brown, G .(1993) *Explaining.* London: Routledge. These books are about primary education but the ideas which they describe are equally applicable at secondary level.

Jackson, K.E. (1975) *The Art of Solving Problems.* London: Heinemann. Describes a systematic way of tackling problems.

Kyriacou, C. (1991) *Essential Teaching Skills.* Oxford: Blackwell. A fuller account of much that is touched on in this chapter.

Marland, M. (1975) *The Craft of the Classroom: a Survival Guide.* London: Heinemann. A practical account of classroom work which, though published some time ago, is still very relevant.

Neill, S. and Caswell, C.(1993) *Body Language for Competent Teachers.* London: Routledge. A useful account of the effect of the teacher's body language and what teachers can learn by observing the body language of their students.

Sotto, E. (1994) *When Teaching Becomes Learning: a Theory and Practice of Teaching.* London:

Cassell Education. Believes strongly in learners being active in the learning process. His approach might be difficult for beginning teachers but the book contains much that is valuable about teaching and learning.

Waterhouse, P. (1983) *Managing the Learning Process*. Maidenhead: McGraw-Hill. Useful material on planning as well as other aspects of teaching.

Wragg, E.C. (ed.) (1984) *Classroom Teaching Skills*. London: Croom Helm/Routledge. Summarizes much useful research on teaching and learning which has a direct practical application.

5

TEACHING AND LEARNING STRATEGIES

The task of the teacher is to facilitate students' learning. This involves seeing students as individuals and being sensitive to their needs and aware of the stage they have reached. This is not easy when you teach a range of classes in the course of the week, but it becomes easier as you continue working in the same school and gradually get to know students and what they can do. It is also important to remember that the way students feel about things helps to determine the extent to which they learn. Their feelings about you as teacher will be important and we have already considered what students look for in a teacher (see pp. 56–7). You also need to consider what they feel about what you are asking them to learn, and how far the learning material links with anything in their own lives.

The HMI publication *Good Teachers* (Department of Education and Science 1985) makes the following points about teaching strategies:

> Good teachers need a variety of approaches and patterns of working and the flexibility to call on several different strategies in the space of one lesson. Sound planning and skilful management are needed to blend class, group and individual work, to pervade a wide range of learning activities, to observe, to solve problems, to offer explanations and to apply skills and ideas.

Tomlinson (1995: 102) suggests that there are four essential aspects of teaching strategy:

- what the pupils are doing e.g. listening, reading, writing, drawing, designing, interacting with a computer, making, doing practical work, watching, discussing;

- how the class is organized e.g. as a whole class, in groups, in pairs, individual working separately;
- the nature of the pupil task function e.g. information finding, information intake, information recording, analysis, application, evaluation, problem-solving, practising;
- what the teacher is doing e.g. directing, prompting, information giving, explaining, eliciting, questioning, listening, watching, demonstrating.

As a teacher you convey to your students a number of messages which are largely hidden. Teacher expectation is a very important part of student learning. You need to make clear to all students that you expect the best work of which they are capable. You need to consider how you convey this message, not so much in what you say to the whole class but in how you deal with individuals. You need to give the message to each that you have high but realistic expectations of him or her.

It may be helpful to consider how far you give the message that learning is interesting and rewarding, that every student's work is valued, that boys and girls and students of different ethnic backgrounds have equally valuable contributions to make and that students' contributions in lessons are valued, as are questioning and inventiveness on the part of students. You may find it useful to give thought to the way you deal with failure. Do less able students feel that they are failing continually, or do they get a reasonable experience of success? Are you challenging the most able in your classes? Do you use praise sufficiently for good behaviour as well as good work? Students are more likely to be motivated and to learn effectively where they feel that they have some degree of control over their learning and responsibility for it.

Students are also more likely to be motivated if they know where work is going and they see value in the tasks they are being asked to undertake. It is therefore a good idea to start any new piece of work and many individual lessons with a statement of what you are setting out to achieve, so that students can share your objectives. This means that you need to be clear about your aims and objectives. It was suggested in Chapter 4 that it can be useful to state objectives in terms of what students will know and be able to do at the end of the lesson and at the end of a series of lessons dealing with a particular topic. This gives you clear criteria against which you can evaluate your work. Of course, you will, in any lesson, help students to learn things other than those in your stated aims and objectives. You may be helping them to acquire study skills; a chance comment from a student may lead into an explanation or discussion about something you had not planned. A good teacher makes the most of any opportunity to help students to learn, but at the same time keeps an eye on the original plan of the lesson.

Learning is easiest when the material to be learned is part of an overall structure and the learner can see where each piece of learning fits in. In the first instance your overall programme is a structure, and you can talk to students about what your long-term plans contain and subsequently tell them about each new piece of learning, so that they are clear as to what it is they are trying to do. The more you can present their learning as a series of identifiable objectives which they can see themselves achieving, the more they are likely to be motivated.

Structuring is more than this, however. Students are learning to structure their own learning and also learning the structures of the different subjects they encounter in school. The ability to sort and classify what is being learned is an important study skill, and you will help the development of this ability by the way you present material and ask questions about it. If you always do the structuring for students they will not learn the skills of structuring for themselves. You need to give them a lot of help in doing this. It may be helpful to discuss with them the best way to set about learning a particular aspect of work. When they have worked on a topic it is a good idea to discuss with them, both as a group and individually, how best to put in order the material they have collected. It may be helpful to teach them first how to make a diagram in which the various points they want to put into their work are jotted down and linked by arrows and lines. They can go on from this to make a flow chart, which puts the material into logical order. They can then use this knowledge in a similar way to plan essays.

Your personal style as a teacher will gradually lead you to prefer some teaching approaches to others, but every teacher needs to use a variety of approaches, varied to meet the interests of the students and the topic being taught.

When you consider approaches it is important to give thought to the extent of student experience of the area of work you plan to introduce. We have already noted that students understand the language you use and the things you refer to only if they can bring comparable experience to the situation. You therefore need to start planning for any new work by considering what experience the students have on which you can draw, and whether they will have an understanding of the new language you want to use. In this context you may need field work in some subjects or a range of examples or practical work, so that work is based on genuine experience.

Kyriacou (1986: 117) makes the following point about teaching methods:

> The biggest single danger facing teachers is to slip into an informing mode of teaching when such a mode is not the most effective for the intended objectives of the lesson. Indeed, the fact that pupils learn more effectively by doing rather than listening indicates that a greater emphasis should be given to pupil involvement and activity across the curriculum than is typical at present.

We use the word 'learn' for several different activities. Sometimes we are asking students to acquire knowledge, perhaps involving memorizing something; sometimes we are concerned with their understanding of a concept; sometimes we are talking about learning a skill. Students need to know how to tackle all three when required.

Tomlinson (1995: 96) defines knowledge as 'a more or less lasting representation of reality. Humans may possess it in a variety of forms (e.g. visual, verbal, concrete, symbolic). When it is knowledge of processes "how things work", in some domain, we tend to call it understanding.' Of concepts, he says, 'Concepts involve identifying and dealing with things, events or abstractions as members of categories or groups. They involve and enable generalizations.' Skills are more obviously about knowing *how* to do something. The National Curriculum demands learning in all three areas.

Secondary school students still need help with ways of memorizing information. Most people find this easiest when the things to be remembered make sense or can be grouped or classified in some way or associated with something else. Learning to spell correctly, for example, involves learning to group words with similar spelling and looking for relationships between them, looking for associations to help memory and writing as well as saying the words. A phrase like 'only one "c" is necessary' will stay in the mind and help the student remember how to spell this word.

Where understanding is concerned, grouping, seeking patterns and structuring learning become essential. Work that asks students to put things in order of priority or to select out things which go together or contrast with one another, or involves flow charts or other forms of graphic layout, contributes to the ability to learn and understand.

The amount people learn from listening to someone talking is limited, though it is still a valid and important form of learning. We learn most fully when we do something for ourselves. Part of the art of teaching is therefore to devise ways in which students have to act on material, finding out from making observations or seeking knowledge from resources of various kinds, including books. Students also need variety in the teaching methods used if they are not to become bored.

There is a need in many subjects to provide practice in some aspect of the work, especially when skills are being learned. You need to think up a variety of ways of offering practice. Quite often the tasks you ask students to undertake will provide the kind of practice they need, as well as having a wider aim. In subjects like mathematics and languages and in spelling you may need to provide practice for its own sake, so that students become proficient in necessary skills. Sometimes it is possible to motivate by making something of a game or competition of this. Computers can also provide motivation for practice if you have suitable programs. Very often work in pairs will be profitable, with students working together to check each other's learning.

An important part of the role of the teacher is in tutoring individual students. Waterhouse (1983: 110) makes the following comment about this:

It is a sort of 'learning conversation' in which the pupil is being helped to be aware of his own stage of development, and to identify for himself how he might develop his understanding. The teacher's job is to listen, to help the pupil to formulate his own statements, to offer reflection and personal support. The aim is get the 'learning conversation' going on almost entirely inside the pupil's own head, so that he becomes an autonomous learner.

He goes on to stress the importance of listening to students and helping them to articulate their own perceptions. This enables the teacher to understand where the students' thinking has reached and what has still to be done to enable them to reach full understanding. Students also need to feel that the teacher values what they have to say.

Secondary schools now offer students some opportunities for negotiating their work with their teacher, particularly in subjects where examinations involve course work. This is demanding for the teacher as well as for the student. Collins (1986) suggests that 'The teacher's role is to listen carefully, translate and clarify, summarize and recapitulate, and avoid criticism or invalidation.' He also suggests that it is important to make the parameters of the discussion clear, so that you both know what is happening. It may be helpful to start with brainstorming and go on to discuss some of the ideas suggested. The discussion should end with some form of contract which sets out what the student is going to do and the time scale within which he or she has to work. It is helpful if the student is clear about the criteria by which the work will be assessed.

INDEPENDENCE IN LEARNING

An important aim for secondary schools is to make students independent learners who are able to learn without a teacher by the time they leave school. In practice this is not very often achieved, but tomorrow's adults are likely to have to learn afresh at many stages of their lives.

Study skills

If students are to become independent learners it is essential that school teaches them the skills of study. These vary from one subject to another and this means that while some skills are general to a number of subjects, many need to be taught as part of subject learning. All teachers in the secondary school need to consider the extent to which students are becoming independent learners in their subject. New technology makes study skills even more important, because if you have a world of knowledge to choose from, how you seek it and what you do with it becomes as important, as remembering parts of it.

The Schools' Council publication *Information Skills in the Secondary Curriculum* (1980) lists eight questions that a student might ask about a particular piece of work. A working party of teachers in one school listed the particular points that might arise from each question. These are given in parentheses.

- What do I need to do?
  (What do the terms mean? How much time do I have? How much detail is needed? What do I already know? What do I need to know?)
- Where could I go?
  (People, libraries, museums, publications, fieldwork, observation, etc. How accessible are these sources? Which is appropriate to the topic?)
- How do I get to the information?
  (Framing questions to ask people. Classification schemes, guides, using a database)
- How shall I use the resources?
  (Indexes, subheadings, appendices, etc. Children must be taught reading skills, such as scanning for facts and reviewing, visual literacy, aural literacy and audio-visual literacy)
- What should I make a record of?
  (What is important? Recording as notes, tabulating, recording, making diagrams, memorising etc. Organising notes)
- Have I got the information I need?
  (A time for reflection, analysis and evaluation)
- How should I present it?
  (Essay, report, talk, model, audio-visual presentation, description)
- What have I achieved?
  (Evaluate)

(Schools Council 1980: 50)

The working party that produced the suggestions in this list believed that the skills could only be taught successfully by a mixture of analysing the processes and carefully planned tasks, which ensured that all the skills were covered in a relevant manner.

The following is a list of skills that students need to acquire if they are to be capable of learning independently. It can be helpful to go down a list of this kind and consider where, in the work you plan, these skills will be developed and whether, by presenting things in a slightly different way, you can increase the abilities of students to study independently. Students need to acquire the ability to:

- plan a project or an enquiry;
- make judgements and hypotheses about what is planned;
- collect information from a variety of sources, including first-hand observation, discussion with other people, information on computer, books and other resources;
- make notes from observation, discussion, information on computer, books and other resources;
- interpret and use graphic and symbolic data, such as charts, graphs, diagrams, maps, pictures, photographs, databases, spreadsheets;
- evaluate the material which has been collected in the light of the original plan or hypothesis, weigh and compare evidence;

- select and organize the material which has been collected for presentation in a variety of forms;
- make presentations in various forms, such as speech, writing, audio or video tape, matching the report to the audience;
- evaluate the presentation.

One aspect of the ability to study independently is the ability to ask questions. In most classrooms the questions tend to be asked by the teacher, and the questions asked by the students are usually straightforward questions about what to do next or where something can be found. There is much to be said for encouraging students to think about the questions they might ask about a particular topic. One way of doing this is to give them a certain amount of information and then ask them to work in pairs or groups of four to think of questions about what they still need to know. The questions can then be the basis of further work, with each pair looking for answers to their questions. You will need to give some time to hearing the questions each group has produced, to ensure that the questions being asked can be explored and to direct them to possible material which will give them the information they need. Some of the questions will require imaginative thinking as well as searches for information.

Language skills

Language is a very important part of the way we think. The HMI document *Good Teachers* (Department of Education and Science 1985: 7) stresses that 'The ways in which teachers use and stimulate their pupils' use of language in the classroom are among the most frequent aspects of teaching skill seen as critical to the success of individual lessons.'

We often think in images of various kinds, but we also think in words. Students' ability to use language therefore has an effect on their ability to think. It is very easy to assume that students have a wider knowledge of language than they actually have. Even when students appear to be able to use specialized subject language, this may not always be an indication of conceptual understanding. The language developing from a student's first-hand experience and personal involvement with subject-specific ideas is far more likely to represent understanding.

Two language skills that need particular training in a number of subjects are the ability to read for a purpose and to take notes. Where possible, students should have access to more than one piece of reading material on any particular topic, so that comparisons can be made, and they will need to be trained to do this. Students need to be able to read carefully, taking in all the points in the text under study. They also need skill in skimming to see if there is anything which is relevant to what they are studying. They can be helped to read carefully by discussion about texts, perhaps looking for the key points in paragraphs and how these relate to the rest of what is said. This can be part of studying for a particular piece of work. This links with note-making where it is the key points that need to be noted. It may be helpful to teach students to make notes in the form of diagrams. Alternatively, it is often helpful to ask students to write headlines for each paragraph or to ask questions which test understanding of the passage.

When you ask students to read something it is important for them to know the purpose of their reading and what they should focus on. They also need to know what they are going to do with the results of their reading. Are they to make notes for another piece of work, summarize what they have read, list keywords and ideas, apply the information to their work, make a precis or a flow chart or do some other activity?

Students need to be able to make inferences from what they have read, identifying what is implied as well as what is said. This needs practice and discussion. Skimming can be practised by asking students to look down a page for where a particular word or point is made, stressing that this does not require them to read the page but to look for the information which is wanted. It also helps to read the first sentence of each paragraph, which usually states what the paragraph is about. All this work can be done as part of subject study.

It is important that students learn to use a library. This means learning to use catalogues, which are now often on computer. Many schools organize this kind of training for library use at an early stage, but subject teachers need to build on it, giving students practice in such skills as using catalogues, indexes and contents lists to find the information they need in the context of their normal work.

Discussion

Discussion may be part of whole-class teaching or a group activity. Dillon (1994: 7) describes discussion as follows:

> Discussion is a form of group interaction, people talking back and forth with one another. What they talk about is an issue, some topic that is in question for them. Their talk consists of advancing and examining different proposals over the issue. The proposals may be various understandings, facts, suggestions, opinions, perspectives, experiences and the like. These are examined for their contribution towards resolving the issues.
>
> As people talk and relate in this way, they begin to form together new, more satisfying answers to their question. For instance, they come to a better understanding, a new appreciation, a wiser judgement, a firmer resolve.

It is helpful if you discuss with students some of the rules of good discussion. Secondary school students should already be aware of the need to take turns in speaking, and you may need to impress on them the importance of listening to one another, considering and respecting different points of view and keeping to the point. Some individuals need to be careful not to go on for too long and take over the discussion. Students need to be clear that the whole process is about helping them to understand the topic under discussion and get into the habit of asking questions themselves as part of their learning.

Case study 3

Jenny, as part of her geography teaching plan for the term, selected the part of Key Stage 3 which says that students should be taught the reason for the location, growth and nature of individual settlements.

She decided to ask her students to work in groups as people who had come from another country a long time ago and were looking for a place to settle. Transport at the time was only by horse and boat. The country was wild and they didn't know whether any local inhabitants would be friendly. They were to decide on what kind of place they would need.

The groups came up with most of the answers she was hoping for. They considered the need for defence, transport, trading, good land for growing crops and herding animals, suitable materials for building houses and some other points. She was then able to ask them to apply this thinking to a particular town and consider why it had grown up in a specific place. This involved studying the map and asking questions about the history of the town.

In whole-class discussion you need to be very welcoming to the comments made, sometimes by smiling and making a welcoming comment and sometimes by weaving what a student has said into the picture that is being built up. You may do this by making a comment like, 'That confirms the point John was making', or you may try to extend the discussion by saying something like, 'That's an interesting point. Does anyone disagree with it?'

Students start to make learning their own when they have to put it into words. In discussion they have to think about what they are learning in order to express their views, and this should make it a good way of learning, providing that the question under discussion is clear and the outcomes are used as building blocks for further learning.

Dillon (1994: 35) quotes a set of aims for group discussion identified by a group of physics teachers. These could apply equally well in almost every subject area:

- to help students communicate as physicists, knowing the language, standards and structures of knowledge in physics;
- to provide practice in the application of principles;
- to encourage the development of critical standards and a questioning attitude towards evidence;
- to extend the range of ideas available to an individual;
- to help students appreciate that physics is about people;
- to provide opportunities for the critical examination of individual and group assignments;
- to encourage familiarity with significant achievements and achievers in physics.

We might add that discussion increases self-confidence and the ability to think and put one's thoughts into words. It also teaches the ability to argue and to respect the points of view of others. It is a good preparation for adulthood, where discussion in groups is part of the working life of many people.

At the level of class rather than group discussion, Wood and Wood (1988) found that students generally responded at greater length and with more information when the teacher made a statement rather than a question. They gave more of their own ideas and questions and were more speculative.

The arrangement of the classroom has an important influence on class discussion. Most people find discussion difficult when they cannot see the faces of those who are contributing. Ideally, you need tables arranged in a horseshoe or circle for good class discussion to take place.

GROUPING FOR LEARNING

As a teacher, you have a choice of the way you group students for learning, which affects the strategies for teaching and learning that you employ. You can teach them as a whole class; you can group them in various ways; you can arrange work in pairs or individually; you can use any combination of these. Each of these types of organization has advantages and disadvantages and is appropriate for some aspects of work. You need to make some use of all of them.

Whole-class teaching

A high proportion of secondary school teaching tends to consist of exposition and questioning involving the whole class. Questioning is an efficient and economical way of eliciting what students know already, on which you can build. Exposition can be a good way of stimulating and interesting students in a new topic or directing their attention and getting work organized. You may choose to use this opportunity to tell a relevant story or personal account, give students an 'advance organizer' of new subject matter or provide a framework for the work to come.

When you are teaching the whole class, it is important to make eye contact with individual members of the class so that all the students feel that what you are saying concerns them. You need to be constantly scanning the class so that they all feel involved and so that you spot any sign of a student not attending.

It is particularly important to think how you will begin a lesson, because this is the point at which you may or may not capture attention. It is also important to have everything ready for whatever activity you want to use to follow your opening, so that the transition from one activity to the next is smooth.

The problem with whole-class teaching is that every class has students of varied ability, and this will be particularly the case where the class is officially of mixed ability. This means that you need to choose language that will be understood by the majority rather than challenging the most able. It also means that there will probably be those who haven't understood what you have been saying, and they will need help on an individual basis at a later stage in the lesson. You may need to talk to the most able students and encourage them to go further in their work than you have suggested for the majority.

When you are setting work to follow your opening you need to consider whether to ask everyone to do the same work or whether to differentiate and give rather different work to different groups of students, designed to match their ability but leading to the same end. An alternative is to set a topic that is open-ended and can be dealt with at different levels. Another possibility is to follow the opening with group work, which can be in mixed-ability groups.

There is likely to be less misbehaviour in whole-class teaching but any that does occur is serious because everyone is aware of it. There is also the danger that students will lose attention if the session goes on for too long.

At the end of a piece of work a mixture of talk and questioning is a good way of drawing together what has been learned, summing up, generalizing, filling gaps and questioning understanding. It is also a sensible approach for giving instructions on safety or organization in a situation where it is important that everyone understands the same thing.

Exposition

Exposition has to be good if it is to capture interest. This means that it needs careful preparation. You need to find a way of making notes about your exposition for yourself that are usable in the classroom situation. One way of doing this is to make notes on overhead projector transparencies which you can show to the students as you talk to them. These have the advantage that you can file them and keep them for another occasion.

Exposition is likely to be more interesting if you can give examples of what you are talking about which are relevant to the students' own lives. In preparing your exposition make sure you have included plenty of examples that you can quote as you go along. Your approach needs to give an example of structure, so that students can see a pattern in what you are saying. This will help them to remember. It should have a logical sequence, with one section leading on naturally to the next.

It is important to keep exposition reasonably short. The length of time for which students are able to attend to teacher talk is limited, and the actual learning happens once the students start to work on the material you are offering. Sotto (1994) suggests that six minutes is about the maximum that teachers should allow themselves for talking to the whole class. This is perhaps a little drastic and older students can, of course, listen profitably for longer than this, but it is a reminder that attention to the teacher talking is limited in duration unless the material is exceptionally interesting. Fontana (1994) is perhaps rather more realistic when he suggests that a good rule of thumb is that students can take about a minute to a minute and a half of teacher talk for each year of their age.

Demonstration

Your subject may include an element of demonstration. You might want to demonstrate a skill or a safety measure. Important aspects to remember are as follows.

- Make sure the group to which you demonstrate is of a size which enables everyone to see clearly and ask questions. You also need to be able to check with them that they have understood what they have seen. It is better to do more than one demonstration than to take on too big a group.
- What you say as you work is important to the students trying to remember that stage in the demonstration. The language helps to fix the activity in students' minds. It may be helpful to have an overhead projector transparency available with the steps written out, so that students can consult this when they come to undertake the task for themselves.
- Do not do too much at once. It is better to do a series of short demonstrations than one very long one, which some students may forget.
- Emphasize safe working practices and warn students of any dangers.

Questioning

It can be only too easy to deal with questions in such a way that the class plays the game of 'guess what the teacher is thinking' rather than thinking for themselves. This happens if you tend, in responding to students' replies to questions, to twist what they say to your own ends on too many occasions, or have a fixed answer in your mind and are not prepared to accept responses which differ from this but which may be valid. It is important really to listen to the responses students give. It is all too easy to have your mind on the next question and to give limited attention to what a student says.

When you are planning questions you need to be clear about the purpose of each question you ask. The overall purpose of asking questions is to get students thinking. There are many ways in which researchers have classified questions, but one useful classification (Morgan and Saxton 1991) classifies questions as those which elicit information, those which shape understanding and those which press for reflection and demand intellectual and emotional commitment by challenging the individual to think critically and creatively. It may be a good idea to look at this classification and consider whether the questions you plan to ask involve all three categories.

It is wise to prepare questions carefully before the lesson and to think of them as a series leading to understanding of particular points. There is a tendency for teachers to use questions which elicit information a great deal and to make too little use of the other kinds of questions. A question like 'What do you think will be the effect of global warming?' or 'Why are people concerned about the rain forests being cut down?' demands reasoning on the part of students and can be answered at a variety of levels. Other questions likely to lead to thoughtful responses are those which require students to use evidence to reach conclusions or apply rules and principles to specific instances. You might ask them to use their imagination or solve problems.

Your treatment of student responses is important. When you work with a new class they will be listening to the way you receive ideas and responses, and your response to them will determine the extent to which they are prepared to risk answering your questions fully or putting forward ideas. In particular, the way you deal with wrong answers is important. You may be able to lead a student giving a wrong answer through further questions to the right answer, or say something which is encouraging before saying that the answer isn't quite right. You also need to make encouraging comments in reply to right answers or partially right answers.

You may want to follow up a response with more probing questions, perhaps leading to some of the thinking you are looking for. However, if you do this too often students will be chary of responding, because they are worried about the further demand on them that you will make. It is all a question of keeping things in the right balance.

Purkey (1978) found that teachers waited only one second for students to answer questions they posed. When waiting time was increased, students gave longer answers, more students volunteered answers, more questions were asked by students and their responses were more analytical, creative and evaluative. There would seem to be a strong case for waiting a little longer for replies.

Students need to be encouraged to ask questions that go beyond the level of asking about something they have not understood, to asking speculative questions and questions that require thought. Barnes and Todd (1977) found that students who worked in small group discussion without the teacher present, generated more exploratory questions, hypotheses and explanations than when the teacher was working with them. It is valuable to think of ways in which students can be encouraged to ask questions.

You need to give thought to the way you set about selecting students to answer questions. If you stand in front of the class you see students in a V-shaped pattern in front of you (see Figure 5.1). It is very easy to ask questions only of those students who come within the shaded triangle, and to omit the others. If you stand well back it is easier to see everyone and avoid the temptation of confining the discussion to those in the shaded part of the diagram. It is worth remembering that students who are keen to learn tend to fill up the front rows in the middle. The less enthusiastic go to the sides and the back.

It is usually wise to pose a question to the whole group without looking at any particular student, and then to decide whom to ask to answer it. If you pick the student first, the rest of the class feel they can relax because they are not being asked the question, although there will be occasions when you choose a student to answer a question to recall his or her attention to the work in hand. It is also easy to ask the same students to answer questions every time, often because they are the keen ones or those you know need to be kept involved. You may find you have a tendency to ask boys to answer more often than girls or the brighter students more often than the slower ones. It is not really possible to keep a check on those students you ask for yourself, but one

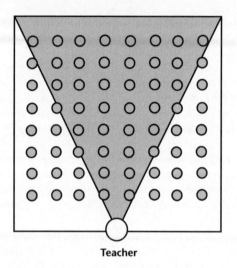

Teacher

Figure 5.1 Classroom view

or two students will enjoy keeping a record for you and this may be a valuable thing to do upon occasion.

Group work

A great deal of adult work involves groups working together, and there is much to be said for some work in groups in the classroom. There are two basic ways in which you can use group work. One form of grouping makes it possible to match work to students of different abilities. Here it is a matter of forming small groups of similar ability or achievement, perhaps teaching them in groups while the rest of the class work on other tasks and then providing them with work matched to their ability.

A different approach to grouping is when students are grouped for cooperative work. This helps them to develop socially and to learn the skills of working with others to an agreed end, very necessary skills for adult life. Dunne and Bennett (1990) make the following points about group work in the primary school. They are equally applicable to the secondary school.

> Cooperatively achieved success is the foundation of learning and development irrespective of subject area. The foundation of the cooperatively achieved success is based on talk; talk is central to social development and to cognitive growth and the two are closely intertwined.
>
> In discussion children test out ideas, in explaining children have to structure their knowledge and find words that will be understood by other children; in arguing they have to make their own opinions known as well as justifying them.
>
> (Dunne and Bennett 1990: 8)

Collins (1986: 46) suggests that monitoring the progress of individuals is easier for the teacher in a group work situation because he or she is free to move around the class and listen to what people have to say. He also notes that 'Students who are shaping their own learning process in groups are likely to discuss dimensions to the task which were not foreseen by the teacher.' Group work is particularly valuable as part of social education, although its main purpose may be learning in other subject areas. Collins (1986: 46) points out that

> Individuals have to learn to adopt helpful roles. They have to learn to listen, to express ideas clearly, to settle disputes and reach consensus. They have to learn how to give and receive support. They may have to learn some formal roles, such as chairing or being secretaries. They will certainly have to learn how to proceed by agreement in the face of differing personalities, values and abilities.

Case study 4

Karen was in her first year of teaching and was convinced by her training of the value of collaborative group work. However, when she tried to do some group work with a year 7 history class, the situation quickly got out of hand, with everyone talking at the same time.

She discussed this problem with her mentor, who suggested that she should work towards group work in a gradual way, starting with work in pairs and then fours. They also agreed that the students needed a very specific task and, since the current work was on castles, they concluded that the task might be to design a castle. This would involve considering the people who would live in it and what they would need, particularly in a seige.

Karen spent some time in the next lesson drawing out from the students the need to listen to each other. She then asked them to name the parts of the castle and she listed these on the board. She next suggested that they work in pairs, listing the people who would live in the castle, what they would need for their everyday lives and what they would need in a seige.

When they had done this she suggested that they turned their chairs round to make groups of four and exchanged information about the lists they had made. She reminded them of the importance of listening to each other. They could then go on to make a plan of a castle which provided all the facilities they had listed.

This was much more successful and she was able to make an exhibition of the plans they had drawn. It also revealed gaps in their knowledge, both while they were working and in the finished work, and she was able to discuss some of these.

Group work, like most other classroom activities, needs careful planning. You need first to think about the particular tasks you want the groups to undertake. If you are using grouping to provide for students of different abilities, this will be a matter of providing rather different routes to the same ends for the different groups, and the work will be individual.

If you are concerned with cooperative group work, groups may be asked to discuss something and come up with statements, questions or some other cooperative piece of work or to solve a problem. They may be asked to plan and work together on a topic to be presented to the class in some way at a later stage. Groups might be asked to compare two accounts of the same event, or place in the correct order a text which has been broken up into separate sentences on individual pieces of card. They could devise questions or a test on the work they have been studying. Group work may involve individuals doing some research for the group and presenting their findings; working together on a problem; brainstorming for ideas to tackle a task or for approaches to a problem; discussing a piece of text and trying to decide on its meaning and implications; producing a report of some kind on work undertaken; and many other tasks. Groups are likely to be particularly productive when they follow some experience which has stimulated the students, who then want a chance to discuss their experience.

You need to think about how you will group students, particularly if you are grouping for cooperative work. The first task is to make a decision about group size. If the group is too big some people can opt out. Five would seem to be an ideal size from some points of view, but is not easy to arrange if you are working in a situation where students normally sit in pairs. From this point of view, groups of four are the easiest to arrange, since in a formally arranged room they can be formed by getting pairs of students to turn round and work with the pair in the tables behind them.

If you wish to group according to ability, students will have to move to different parts of the room. This needs careful planning. It is appropriate when you want the work to be individual but different for each group. Ability grouping also allows you to teach a group at a time at a level which matches the students' ability, but you will need to ensure that other students have work they can do without reference to you. It should be noted that it is easy for ability grouping to become a self-fulfilling prophecy, because students recognize that less is expected of them if they are in a low-ability group and perform accordingly. You need to watch this. If you are grouping by ability for a situation where students do individual work, the size of group does not really matter. It may, for example, be a good idea to divide the class into three, with each group having work which matches the ability of its members.

You can group according to friendship, allowing students to decide for themselves which group they are in. This has some advantages, in that students are working with people with whom they wish to work, but you may find that this results in all the trouble makers being in one group. There may also be isolates who are not welcome in any group.

Dunne and Bennett (1990) suggest that collaborative work is more effective if each group contains some really able students who are able to give a lead to the thinking of the group. Although this is a suggestion for group work in primary schools, in practice it applies equally well at later stages. The less able students ought to be spread round the groups. This suggests that an effective form of grouping for cooperative work is probably one where you deliberately place students in groups that you think will work. This is easiest to do when you know your students really well. It means moving students about the room rather than simply using the groups of four suggested above. It may be best to start with fours where students are seated and observe what happens, perhaps gradually moving to different groupings so that students have the experience of working with a variety of different people.

You need to plan for the way you will ask everyone to move into groups. This may mean moving furniture and you need to think out exactly how this is to be done if you want to avoid chaos. The experience of Karen, described in case study 4 (p. 73), in working towards grouping by starting with pairs is worth considering.

In a mixed school you need to make a decision about whether to have groups of mixed gender. Generally speaking, younger students tend to object to this but this changes as they grow older, and there are some advantages in mixing boys and girls in that they contribute differently to groups, although you will need to be sure that neither boys nor girls are dominating the discussion.

If you want collaborative group work to be successful, you need to consider whether your students need some training in group work skills. They may need encouragement to listen to each other carefully, to question or challenge an argument without being aggressive. They may also be helped by being given suggestions about patterns of working, the stages through which they might work and some of the questions they might consider. You should give clear instructions about the time available and the need to keep the noise level low.

Group leaders may need training in leading a group, so that everyone contributes. They need to learn some simple rules of procedure and may need to learn to encourage group members to contribute, how to obtain ideas from the group, how to share out the tasks and pace the work, encouraging and supporting everyone and then helping the group to see how the pieces fit together. They also need to help the group keep its goals in sight.

Group work is more difficult to assess than class work or individual work. Dunne and Bennett (1990: 36) quote a teacher as suggesting that to assess the work of a group, a teacher needs to consider:

- their ability to cooperate;
- their understanding of the task and how to implement its completion;
- the suitability of the task for their needs;
- how the working group gels and how best its composition may be altered where necessary;

- who is helping whom in each group and if the help is aiding the understanding of the task;
- how suitable the resources available to learners are and how effectively
  the resources are used.

There are problems with group work, as with any form of organization. Less
able students may opt out or hold up the work of the group. Able students
may feel that they are doing more than their fair share. The group may find
ways of simplifying the task to make it easier to do and less valuable, especially if they fail to see the point of it in the first place. Individuals may come to
feel rejected if their contributions are not welcomed. These are all problems
for the teacher to look out for and try to counter.

Paired work

The easiest form of group work to organize is work in pairs. This does not
usually require any changes of seating and no time is wasted getting people
into groups. It provides the opportunity to talk through what is being learned
and can be valuable in many ways. Students can be asked to discuss problems,
prepare questions or statements and undertake tasks, as well as the kind of
paired tutoring discussed on page 79. The only problem for the teacher is that
of being sure that what is discussed is relevant to the task in hand, and to some
extent this can be taken care of by the demands made for products as a result
of discussion.

Individualized and resource-based work

There is a sense in which a great deal of work is individual in most classrooms,
in that the teacher sets tasks for students which they do according to their
ability. However, the phrase 'individualized work' in this context refers to work
which is designed to match the needs of particular students, a situation in
which different students may be doing different work or interpreting an open-
ended question differently. The extent to which individualized work is possible tends to depend to some extent on the subject as well as on the size of the
class. In mathematics, for example, students may work on individual programmes if you have suitable materials for this, with occasional group or class
teaching. If you work this way it is important to see that students also get the
stimulus of working in a group or whole class. In other subjects this may be
more difficult, and a subject like modern languages relies heavily on work in
a class or group.

Individualized work usually requires materials designed for this purpose and
worksheets, computer programs and other resources can gradually be built up
over a period, so that you have a variety of tasks available for particular pieces
of learning. Resources can include audio and video tapes, slides, cuttings from

magazines and newspapers, maps, graphs and diagrams as well as actual objects. As you gather these you need to work out a storage and filing system for them, so that they are easily retrievable when you need them. If you make an index as you go along this need not necessarily be too difficult a task. The index might include brief details of each item and an indication of the topics and students for which it may be suitable. Ideally, your filing system should be usable by students as well as yourself, and this means that you need to code each piece of material as you add it to the collection so that it can easily be returned to the right place and found again when it is needed. One way of doing this is to use coloured sticky spots for different classifications of material, and perhaps a number.

If the teachers in a department set out to search for and produce materials and share them, everyone can have a range of suitable resources for different teaching topics. This enables you to match tasks to individual students and to offer students a choice of activity.

Resource-based learning requires the students to have the necessary skills to work in this way. Davies (1978) suggests that the students need to be able to extract information showing a grasp of meaning, synthesize information from several sources and assess and interpret information for relevance and accuracy. These are advanced skills and should be developed in the process of training students to read effectively and study independently. Students will also need to be able to access and use information on computer. However, you can plan resource-based work to match any level of ability. Less able students will need to be directed to specific information and helped and guided in abstracting what they need to know from it, gradually building up their skills.

In a number of situations you might want to make work cards identifying the tasks that individuals or groups are to undertake. It pays to do this as carefully as possible, bearing in mind that good work cards can be used again and you can build up a collection of material for future use. Waterhouse (1983: 23–4) offers the following advice about making work or task cards:

- Avoid as much as possible the fact extraction – fact reproduction type of task.
- Aim to develop higher order intellectual skills: application of know-ledge, analysis, problem solving, evaluation.
- Allow the pupil as much decision making as possible.
- Aim to develop organizing skills.
- Examine the language of the task card critically for ambiguities and confused writing.
- Make sure that the language of the task card is well within the reading competence of the target pupil.
- Guide the pupil towards an end product which will be satisfying in itself.
- Make sure that the end product of the pupil's work will prove to be self-explanatory when the work is retrieved at a later date.

- Use models to suggest ways of tackling a task and to suggest ways of presenting the finished work.
- Always test a task card before use.
- Make a note of confusions and difficulties when the card is in use, so that changes can be made.

The advent of computers has made it much more possible to provide for individualized work and we are gradually seeing software produced which is designed to discover what the student already knows and to take the learning on from there.

Individualized work is particularly needed when a student has missed work and needs to catch up. If you make a habit of checking who is present in your classes, you will be in a position to suggest ways in which anyone who was absent can make good the work he or she has missed.

Individualized work is less easy to assess than work done as a class. Davies (1978) suggests that the teacher builds into the work points at which the student should refer to the teacher. This will enable you to assess how far the student has achieved what you intended. He also suggests that your records should include a note of the items you want the student to complete, the skills you want him or her to acquire, with some indication of the level of competence being achieved and comments to remind you of any problems. This is very demanding for the teacher. You will also be able to assess by observing how students are working and talking with individuals and by looking at the outcomes of the work.

Individualized learning is not easy for the teacher and needs to be built up gradually, as you develop materials and help the students to develop the skills of study. It is easiest to start by differentiating work for groups of students and then gradually making this work more individual as you get to know the students and their preferred learning styles and interests. It is important to build in time goals – points by which parts of the task are to be finished.

Other strategies

Role play, drama and simulation offer interesting ways of exploring some aspects of learning. Many historical and geographical situations can be studied and then discussed from the points of view of different people in the situation. For example, a discussion in which the students each play the part of different people on a new housing estate, considering the siting of the primary school, might give rise to some interesting discussion and help students to see things from different points of view. Some historic houses offer the opportunity for students to take part in role plays in which the students play the part of people living at another time.

Another approach to role play might be to work in pairs, with one person acting as a reporter or perhaps a psychologist interviewing the other in a particular role. For example, a psychologist might interview the nurse in *Romeo and Juliet* about the part she played and how she felt about it. This might be described as experiential learning. Kyriacou (1986: 75) describes this as follows: 'Experiential learning involves providing pupils with an experience which will totally and powerfully immerse them in "experiencing" the issue which is being explored, and will result in influencing their cognitive understanding, and also their affective appreciation (involving feelings, values and attitudes).'

Another valuable way of working is to use paired tutoring. Here parts of the class learn different sections of the work and then work in pairs to teach each other what they have learned. This can be done within one class or it can be carried out with an older and a younger class or with two parallel classes. Goodlad and Hirst (1990: 6) make the following point about the advantage to those doing the tutoring: 'Tutors learn by reviewing and finding meaningful use of subject matter, filling in gaps in their own education, consolidating learning or learning through a process of reformulation.' They suggest that peer tutoring is particularly valuable for less able readers, who can be given the task of tutoring younger children. This gives them confidence and reinforces their own learning.

A pair of classes differing in age might well work together on something like an environmental study, with the students in the older class each having a 'student' from the younger class. This provides 'teachers' on a one-to-one basis and the achievement of the older students may be judged from how well the younger ones have learned. This can also be organized within a pair of classes of the same age group, with each class taught something, which they then have to teach the other class. Similar work can be done in the same class, with half the students preparing one part of the work independently and the other half of the class preparing a different part of the work. The two are then paired and each teaches the other what he or she has learned. The motivation involved in this is considerable. However, it is important to check what has been learned by both tutors and learners. This approach depends upon the way the timetable is structured.

Students may work in groups on a particular project, finding out different aspects of the topic and going on to present it to the whole class in some form. They should be helped and encouraged to spend time working out carefully the structure of the project before deciding how work will be divided up.

Brainstorming is often useful, particularly in group work. Here students might be asked to think of as many questions as they can about a topic which could be explored, or they might see how many ways they can think of for exploring the topic. The idea of brainstorming is that people think quickly of ideas and do not stop to consider whether they are possible or not at the early stage, but go on to consider them more thoroughly when they have a lot of ideas. Someone will need to note the ideas down in each group.

MIXED-ABILITY TEACHING

You may find yourself in a school which works on the basis of mixed-ability teaching, perhaps just for year 7 but possibly for later years as well. This requires different approaches from teaching an ability group, although many of the techniques which work with mixed-ability classes are equally effective with other groups, and even in a set grouped by ability the range may be quite wide.

Kelly (1974: 3) comments about mixed-ability teaching: 'There is no denying that teaching in this kind of situation, although more rewarding, is a much more difficult, demanding and complex job than teaching classes that are relatively homogeneous in terms of ability.' Reid *et al.* (1987) discovered in their research that teachers in their first year found mixed-ability teaching particularly difficult and teachers with ten or more years of experience disliked it as a form of organization. Other teachers varied in their views according to subject, with English and humanities tending to be enthusiastic about it and mathematics and modern languages teachers finding it difficult to operate because of the nature of their subjects. Teachers also appeared to like it better the more they did of it.

If you teach a mixed-ability group this places limitations on the work you can do as a whole class. It is still a good way of starting work and drawing it together at the end, and a good situation for discussion. Reid *et al.* found that English and humanities teachers felt that the range of experience in the mixed-ability class was particularly valuable for discussion. What is much more difficult is to teach topics which have a logical structure that must be understood or to develop an understanding of concepts through whole-class teaching. These aspects of work require both individual resource-based work using worksheets, tapes or computer programs and opportunities for discussion and work in pairs and small groups.

Another problem for the new teacher is that good mixed-ability teaching requires the teacher to know the students well, and this takes time. Less able students will identify themselves fairly quickly and it may be wise to get some information about those with serious difficulties from other teachers. The very able need material which extends them.

Sands and Kerry (1982) suggest that teachers with mixed-ability classes need to be flexible, employing a range of teaching strategies, varying the style and pace of lessons and using a variety of resources. They also need to be aware of the needs of students and able to handle a variety of activities at the same time. They quote a survey of teachers' opinions about successful teachers of mixed-ability classes, which suggests that such teachers prepare thoroughly, are knowledgeable and enthusiastic about their subject matter, ask effective questions, are able to take and use feedback from students, take risks and innovate in their teaching and admit mistakes and learn from them. They are also good at devising resources and accept students as individuals.

Ingleson (1982: 106) stresses that 'The recognition of the differences between individual pupils should be reflected clearly in the teaching styles and approaches.' He suggests that it is important to consider not only academic ability but also personality and temperament. 'A willingness to look honestly at the needs and talents of the children and to modify presentation and style accordingly, implies both commitment and open-mindedness' (p. 107).

The case study of Karen on page 73 and that of Jenny on page 67 describe open-ended approaches. Case study 5 describes work at different levels.

If you find that you need to make new material, try to make it in a form which you will be able to use on a future occasion, so that you gradually build up a collection of material which meets the needs of a mixed-ability class. Avoid complex sentences when making worksheets for the less able and give explanations of technical words and unfamiliar words. This helps to extend vocabulary. It is often helpful for less able students if they can answer the questions actually on the worksheet. This can give a sense of achievement. More able pupils can take more in the way of text and more complex language, but it is still important not to crowd the sheet.

Kerry (1982: 100) found that many teachers tackled mixed-ability classes by teaching to just below the middle of the ability range. He also found that

Case study 5

Simon was in his first year as a teacher of geography. One of his year 8 classes posed particular problems for him, as he gradually discovered how wide the spread of ability was within the class. He discussed this with his head of department, who suggested that he used the knowledge he had gained about the students' abilities to divide the class into three broad ability groups. He then devised worksheets at three different levels, each having similar learning in mind. The worksheet for the most able demanded a good deal from the most able students. It involved problem-solving and a high level of reasoning and thinking. The worksheet for the middle group was more structured and less demanding, while still expecting some problem-solving. It included more guidance for the students. The worksheet for the least able group used much simpler language, gave a great deal of guidance and led students through the problem to be solved in some detail.

He then assembled the resources each group would need for the work he had planned, and put some of the printed text for the least able group on audio tape so that they could listen as well as read. This took a lot of careful planning to ensure that there was enough material for everyone. He dealt with this by suggesting that different students started with different tasks so that there was not a rush for the same resources.

In practice he found that this worked quite well, although he still had to do some extra explaining for some of the least able students, and he concluded that he could have been even more demanding of the most able. He made a note of the modifications of the worksheets that he would need if he was to use them again. He concluded that he could, with advantage, use the same worksheets with the other year 8 classes he was teaching.

'Bright students tended to experience dead time from finishing quickly, boredom as a result, loss of interest and some disruption or at best some disenchantment resulting from prolonged lack of interest.' He stresses the need to see that such students acquire study skills so that they are able to progress.

Slower learners will need to acquire study skills, but these need to be built up slowly. They tend to have a more limited span of concentration and need short tasks and much repetition and reinforcement, which can be done while others are working. However, their problems will differ and the better you get to know them the more profitably you will be able to plan work for them.

Checklist 6 – Teaching strategies

- Do I convey enthusiasm for learning and for my subject?
- Are my students interested and involved?
- Did I achieve my objectives?
- Do I make every student feel that his or her work is valued?
- Do my less able students feel that they experience success?
- Am I challenging the most able students?
- Am I providing for students of average ability?
- Am I providing for the less able students?
- Am I helping students to become independent learners?
- Am I using whole-class teaching effectively?
- What are my students gaining from group work?
- Am I making appropriate use of individual and resource-based work?
- Is there enough variety in my teaching methods?
- Is the monitoring and evaluation I am doing adequate?

FURTHER READING

Barnes, D. and Todd, F. (1977) *Communication and Learning in Small Groups.* London: Routledge and Kegan Paul. A useful account of what may be gained from small group work.

Brown, G. and Wragg, E.C. (1993) *Questioning.* London: Routledge. Dunne, E. and Bennett, N. (1990) *Talking and Learning in Groups.* London: Macmillan. Wragg, E.C. and Brown, G. (1993) *Explaining.* London: Routledge. These short practical books have been written for primary school teachers but contain much that is relevant at the secondary stage.

Dillon, J. (1994) *Using Discussion in Classrooms.* Buckingham: Open University Press. Makes a strong case for the value of discussion as a way of learning.

Goodlad, S. and Hirst, B. (1990) *Explorations in Peer Tutoring.* Oxford: Blackwell. A helpful account of peer tutoring and its advantages.

Morgan, N. and Saxton, J. (1991) *Teaching Questioning and Learning*. London: Routledge. Describes questioning as 'the means by which teachers help students to construct meaning'. Suggests ways in which questioning helps students to think.

Sands, M. and Kerry, T. (1982) *Mixed Ability Teaching*. London: Croom Helm. A book about the methods and strategies needed for teaching mixed-ability classes.

Sutton, C. (ed.) (1981) *Communicating in the Classroom*. London: Hodder and Stoughton. The writers in this book take the view that learning becomes effective when the learner has integrated it into what he or she already knows. Each chapter is concerned with ways to do this. Has practical suggestions.

6

CLASS MANAGEMENT

The management of a class of students in a secondary school to enable them to learn well requires a good deal of professional skill. This takes time to acquire, and beginning teachers should not be too depressed when they find that what looks easy in the hands of an experienced teacher works much less well for them. The relationship between teacher and students is a subtle one, which is different with each group. Denscombe (1985: 96) describes the problem of class management as follows:

> In effect, legal and institutional authority give teachers a superior power base yet it is obvious that teacher strategies for control do not operate on a passive body of pupils ... They engage in counter strategies geared towards their own interests in the classroom situation and use ploys to limit the nature and extent of [teacher] control which is feasible in class.

Although the development of skill in class management takes time, there is a great deal that can be learned about it. Waterhouse (1983: 129) suggests that the teacher's image is an important weapon in his or her armoury. The teacher needs to give a serious and firm impression of purpose. This 'is conveyed by being thorough both in one's own contributions and in the demands made on the pupils. This means attention to detail, and an assumption that pupils will take their work seriously and with a sense of responsibility.' The teacher also needs to give an impression of strength and resolution and of a caring adult. There is evidence (Gray and Richer 1988; Fontana 1994) that it is important for teachers to be punctual in arriving at lessons. A late start is an unsatisfactory start.

The Elton Report, *Discipline in Schools* (DES and Welsh Office 1989: 64), makes the following point about the teacher's ability to control what happens in the classroom: 'When a teacher sees behaviour, judges it to be unacceptable and intervenes to stop it, it is the relationship between that teacher and the pupil or pupils involved which will determine the success of the intervention.'

The Report goes on to point out that 'Children have a need to discover where the boundaries of acceptable behaviour lie. It is natural for them to test these boundaries to confirm their location' (p. 65). This means that it is important for teachers to be clear about what they are prepared to allow and confirm the boundaries whenever they are tested. This is not easy for new teachers since they need time to discover what the school finds acceptable as well as what they themselves are prepared to accept. Capel *et al.* (1995: 109) suggest: 'If you do not rise to any bait given by pupils, but respond coolly, calmly, firmly and fairly, the pupils soon become bored with testing you out and get on with the task of learning.'

Good preparation is an essential basis for good class management. You need to know exactly what you intend to do and be prepared for things that might go wrong. Students need to know where they stand and what is coming. Predictability leads to a feeling of security, although an element of surprise from time to time is also a good thing. Suggestions about preparation were given in Chapter 2.

Gray and Freeman (1987: 134) make the rather different point that 'The basic requirement for good order in the classroom is that those involved should understand that it is in their mutual interest to maintain it.' They also suggest that 'Responding to student views in a positive way by full and open discussion of the method of teaching is the best way of dealing with many incipient problems' (p. 143).

It is a good thing to remember that humour in the classroom can relieve tension and that a teacher who can see the humorous side of things is less likely to be stressed in dealing with difficult classes. Students appreciate a teacher who will 'have a laugh' with them. They also appreciate a teacher who will admit mistakes and be prepared to apologize if in the wrong.

Fontana (1994: 4) notes that control is not only based upon 'an enlightened understanding of child behaviour but an understanding by the teacher of *his or her own* behaviour and upon a realization that many of the problems of control that arise in the classroom are a direct consequence of the way in which the teacher acts (or reacts) towards the children concerned.' He suggests (p. 101) that teachers should 'study ways of changing how they present themselves to the child, instead of automatically assuming that it is the child who is at fault and who must therefore be the one to make any changes that appear to be necessary.'

STARTING THE LESSON

Do your best to be in the classroom before students start to arrive. If the pattern in your school is one where students line up outside the classroom until the teacher is ready for the class to come in, stand by the door so that you can see both outside the classroom and inside. Don't get involved with individual queries at this stage, because you need to be seen to be observing what is happening, although you may want to make friendly comments to some students. Keep scanning the class and call to attention anyone who seems to be misbehaving.

If it is the first lesson with this particular group you may want to give instructions about where they should sit. If it is a later lesson you may need to remind them that they should sit in the places they were in before and that you have a record of this. If it is your first lesson with a new group you will need to discuss the rules you want kept in the classroom. You might like to ask students for suggestions about suitable rules or simply spell out the rules you wish to introduce. Wragg (1984: 67) found that experienced teachers introduced some form of rules about the following:

- no talking when the teacher is talking to the whole class;*
- no disruptive noises;
- rules for entering, leaving and moving about the classroom;*
- no interference with the work of others;*
- work must be completed in a specified way;
- pupils must raise their hands to answer, not shout out;*
- pupils must make a positive effort with their work;
- pupils must not challenge the authority of the teacher;
- respect should be shown for property and equipment;*
- rules to do with safety;
- pupils must ask if they do not understand.*

There are more rules here than a teacher would introduce during the first lesson. Rules that might be discussed during the first lesson are marked with an asterisk. Other rules would be introduced at suitable times. For example, rules for completing work can be introduced when work is being set, and safety rules in the main when students are about to do some activity where safety is an issue. Other rules, like not challenging the authority of the teacher, will emerge from the way you deal with situations in which there is a challenge. Generally speaking, rules are better expressed in positive terms. Thus a rule like 'No interference with the work of others' might be better expressed as 'Let other people get on with their work'.

Once you have made the classroom rules clear (perhaps writing them on the board or an overhead projector transparency and getting students to copy them into their notebooks), you must deal firmly with any infringement, reminding the students that these are the rules for this class. It is a good idea to put a copy on a notice board so that you can refer to them when necessary.

Classroom rules might seem much more acceptable to students if you list rules that you will attempt to keep to. For example, you may promise to mark homework promptly or explain the reason for any delay. Neill and Caswell (1993: 101) suggest that

Effective teachers present rules as something above both teacher and child, which both have to obey, or as a bargain which both have to keep to. The situation ceases to be defined as a confrontation between teacher and child, which the child might be able to win or negotiate his way out of; you now appear to be as much bound by the terms of the rules as the child.

Before you start any work, insist on silence and attention. Experienced teachers tend to make a lot of use of eye contact here, looking at students who are not ready and gesturing the need for them to calm down. Another technique is to praise students who are ready and waiting. This is effective with younger students, but some older students find this embarrassing. The persistent trouble maker, in particular, may feel that public praise will damage his or her reputation, but may find a quiet word of praise acceptable and even pleasing. It is useful to agree a signal with the students that when, for example, you clap your hands, you want their attention.

Try to look relaxed and confident as you wait for silence. Avoid nervous gestures and don't be tempted to shout above the noise. Looking confident is something you need to do at all stages. Fontana (1994: 108) suggests that a confident manner includes:

- being unhurried in speech and actions;
- maintaining relaxed and non-threatening eye contact with the class and individuals;
- avoiding nervous mannerisms and gestures;
- being ready to smile at the class as appropriate and join in any reasonable classroom laughter;
- avoiding unjustified antagonism or over-reaction to the children's behaviour.

CLASSROOM CONTROL

Fontana (1985: 3) describes control in the classroom as follows:

[It is] the process of running an organized and effective classroom, a classroom in which the abilities of individual children are given due opportunity for development, in which teachers can fulfil their proper function as facilitators of learning, and in which the children can acquire sensibly and enjoyably the techniques for monitoring and guiding their own behaviour . . . The purpose of classroom control is not that the teacher is thus enabled to assert personal authority and status over the children, but to enable one to work towards a situation in which the exercise of such control becomes less and less necessary.

The Elton Report (DES and Welsh Office 1989) reminds us that the kind of behaviour that most worries teachers is not serious misbehaviour but irritating minor breaches of discipline, such as talking out of turn, hindering other pupils, making unnecessary noises, calculated idleness or work avoidance, not being punctual and getting out of the seat without permission. Teachers much less frequently encountered verbal and physical aggression, aggression towards other pupils and destructiveness.

There are many reasons why students misbehave in the classroom. Sometimes they are bored or find prolonged mental effort too much of a strain. There may be students with low self-esteem when it comes to academic work, and as a result they have poor attitudes to work. A few may be genuinely maladjusted as a result of their backgrounds. Students also misbehave because of their own internal problems. Some may find it difficult to deal with any form of frustration. They may have written off school as something that offers them little, but that can be made more amusing by baiting teachers. They may be part of an anti-school group within the school.

Gray and Richer (1988: 6) found in studying the students who were disruptive that

> as a group they tend to have a lower IQ, poor academic achievement, lower social economic class, a relatively high prevalence of 'neurological' problems, to come from homes where there is marital discord, and from families with financial or housing difficulties, they tend to suffer harsh and/or inconsistent discipline at home from fathers who may have a criminal or psychiatric history.

They also found that such students worked for only 50 per cent of the time compared with the 70 per cent worked by the majority. This meant that their academic achievement continued to be poor and became poorer. In addition, they found that such students lacked social skills and found it difficult to relate to adults. They were not liked very much by their peer group. Gray and Richer suggest that the disruption such students cause arises essentially from their insecurity. They state: 'A prime source of that insecurity is frustration, especially that stemming from a mismatch between the external expectations made of the pupil and his internal self-evaluation' (p. 51). They suggest that an important way of dealing with this is to try to match work to the student whenever possible. 'You must recognize each pupil's starting point, his self-esteem or self-image, and your expectations must relate to that starting point' (p. 52).

Such students may have concluded that they will not succeed in school work and concentrate their attention on entertaining their peers by annoying the teacher. They tend to get labelled as trouble makers and they then tend to try to live up to the label. It is very easy for a teacher to build up an expectation that difficult students will always be difficult and to treat them accordingly, even when their actions are quite innocent and this encourages them to live up to the teacher's expectations. You need to be ready to judge a student's behaviour on its own merits rather than in terms of pre-supposition.

Some students may be bored because they do not understand the work and some because they are highly intelligent and find the pace too slow. Some have found in growing up that the only way they can attract the attention of adults is to be aggressive and demanding. Some have a poor self-image and set themselves low standards. Some have home circumstances that leave them deeply unhappy and unable to concentrate in school.

You need to try to analyse the reasons for misbehaviour and work accordingly. In nearly every case you need to be firm, consistent, supportive and patient. For some students the task is to make them believe in themselves and gradually build up their self-esteem. Slow students may need more help in coping with the work of the classroom, and very able students may need an enriched curriculum, with more demands made upon them. When you are preparing work you should have the needs of the more difficult students in mind as well as those of the able and the majority.

Waterhouse (1983: 126) suggests that in some cases the school may cause problems with students. It

> may give an impression that it cares little for those who are not distinguished intellectually. It may display a distrust of its pupils through a number of minor rules and regulations and in its conventions; it may regularly stifle self-confidence. It may show little respect for the opinions or feelings of its pupils.

If you are in a school where this kind of situation applies you will need to work hard in the classroom to overcome the lack of self-esteem that the school has created.

As students grow older they will demand more independence. You need to be conscious of this and increase the responsibility you offer students as they move up the school. You also need to prepare them to take greater responsibility for their work by building study skills gradually. By the time students reach school leaving age they should be able to learn independently. In practice very few are able to do this, but it is something to aim for.

Good teachers pre-empt misbehaviour by constantly scanning the classroom and noting students who are not doing what they should, and, where appropriate, moving towards them and making eye contact. They move around the classroom, looking particularly for students who are having difficulty and for students likely to misbehave. They are sensitive to the point in a lesson where students are becoming restless with the task they have been given, and they change the activity. They move a student if necessary, stressing that this is in the student's own interest so that he or she can work more effectively.

As a teacher you come with the authority of the school on your side, but you still have to win control so that you can teach effectively. The following points may be relevant.

- Learn names as quickly as possible. It is very difficult to deal with students as individuals if you do not know their names.
- Try to look confident and act as if you expect to dominate the situation. Your tone of voice in issuing instructions can indicate that you expect the instruction to be obeyed without question.

- Deal quickly with any misbehaviour. Making eye contact may be sufficient to stop some misbehaviour, if it is clear from your facial expression that you have seen and do not approve. If this is not effective you may wish to comment or move towards the offender, looking at him or her as you do so. There is some evidence that soft reprimands, made to the individual concerned, are more effective than loud reprimands made so that the whole class can hear.
- Be very clear in demanding the behaviour you want, particularly at points of change of activity. Once you have given students the rules for the classroom deal firmly with any occasion when they are disobeyed, reminding the students that these are the classroom rules.
- When you comment on a student misbehaving, try to make this a comment about what he or she should be doing (e.g. 'John, have you finished your work?') rather than simply a comment about the misbehaviour. This can have a ripple effect on other members of the class.
- Identify the class leaders as soon as possible and work to control them.
- Get to know the students who pose behaviour problems as quickly as you can, and try to analyse their particular problems. In most cases they will have low self-esteem and their lack of success in work will threaten this. Remember that they tend to be insecure and find relationships with adults difficult, and try to be sympathetic to these problems.
- Make sure that everyone has plenty of work to do and that there is something interesting for those who finish early. Idleness can produce disruption.
- Praise those who are behaving well. It is important that praise is merited and sincere.

You may follow all these suggestions and still find that you have students who pose problems. Very often, incidents of misbehaviour require no more than reprimand, perhaps moving towards the student in question and speaking firmly. Make sure you target the right person and avoid anger. The Elton Report found that reasoning with students outside the classroom setting was generally effective for dealing with misbehaviour. When you are discussing what happened try to get the student to reason through to the consequence of his or her actions, with the aim that in future that student will do some reasoning before acting. The better you know the student and the more you are able to identify the causes of the problem, the more you are likely to be successful.

Gray and Richer (1988: 6) found that low rates of disruption were correlated with such factors as emphasis on reward rather than punishment, immediacy of reaction on indiscipline, teachers being approachable about pupils' personal problems, involving pupils in leadership activities, punctuality of teachers and well prepared lessons.

Punishment may be useful but it tends to have a short-term effect. You really need a longer-term strategy that is more positive. There are a number of ideas that have been found to work and you might like to try some of them.

Case study 6

Linda had generally made a very good start to her first year of teaching but in one year 9 class there were several students who gave her a lot of trouble. One boy in particular, Philip, was apparently unable to sit still and concentrate for any length of time and was always disturbing other people.

Linda had heard about behaviour modification at college and decided to give it a try. She kept a note over a week of the times when Philip disturbed others and at the end of the week talked with him about this. He accepted that he disrupted other people's work and agreed to try a scheme whereby he worked for just ten minutes by the clock without getting up or disturbing anyone. Together they set out a record for him to keep when he succeeded in doing this. Linda made a special point of observing him so that she could praise him when he succeeded in working for the agreed time.

It took time for this to work and sometimes he succeeded and sometimes he did not, but he gradually became able to work without disturbing others. As he became more able to do this, he agreed with Linda to try to work for increasing lengths of time.

Behaviour modification

This works on the basis that behaviour is something learned. Some students behave in ways that are inappropriate and need to be helped to learn new ways of behaving. The ideas can be applied to individuals or whole classes. They are based on the premise that 'Behaviours followed by positive reinforcers are likely to increase in frequency' (Wheldall and Merrett 1984: 20).

In case study 6, Linda started by describing to herself the behaviour she wished to change in very specific terms. She described this as 'any interruption of other students' work at times when individual work is in progress'. Philip agreed without much argument that he did interrupt other people's work and that he would have a go at the target she suggested. The exact terms of the target in a particular case depend on the student and what he or she thinks is possible. It would have been possible to set out an agreement in the form of a written contract for the student, which she and Philip both signed. Ideally there should be some reward for this achievement, but praise for achievement is something of a reward in itself and was all that was needed in this case. A letter to parents may form another kind of reward when the new behaviour is really established.

When you are using this approach it is important initially that the required behaviour is rewarded each time it happens. This is not easy to do in a busy classroom. Where progress seems slow, it is necessary to do what is called 'shaping', which involves rewarding behaviour that comes near to what is required.

It is necessary to avoid where possible rewarding with attention the behaviour you want to extinguish. This is not always a reasonable thing to do, but very often bad behaviour is a way of trying to get attention, and if it is rewarded with the teacher's attention it is likely to be repeated, even though the attention is negative. Teachers tend to make more negative than positive remarks about behaviour. Wheldall and Merritt (1984) found that both primary and secondary teachers made disapproving compared with approving remarks about behaviour in a ratio of four to one, while the ratio was virtually reversed in the case of academic work.

If you want to deal with the whole class, similar processes apply. You analyse in detail the problem you are encountering, note how often the problem occurs and discuss this with the class, asking for suggestions about how the problem can be overcome, or you can come up with your own solutions and try them out. If, for example, you have difficulty in settling students down to work, one possible thing to do is to set a kitchen timer to go off every ten minutes and then count those students who are on task. You will probably find that there is increased work on task as a result of this.

Behaviour modification is a subject that raises a good deal of controversy. There are those who feel that it is a comparatively superficial way of dealing with students, since it largely ignores the mental state that may be the cause of the problem. It certainly appears to be an effective way of dealing with some problems. It is probably best used in conjunction with a certain amount of counselling and thought about why a student misbehaves.

Behaviour modification is described in more detail in Wheldall and Merrett (1984) and in a number of the other books listed at the end of this chapter.

Assertive discipline

This American system of classroom control, devised by Canter (1979), involves establishing in agreement with students no more than five rules in the classroom. If these rules are broken, everyone must be able to see this. There is then an escalating scale of no more than five consequences, which might start with a warning and the student's name being written on the board, and ending with a visit to the headteacher and perhaps a letter to parents. There must be many rewards for good work and behaviour, which are handed out liberally, including letters to parents. Rewards should outnumber sanctions.

This might be criticized for the same reasons as behaviour modification, but schools that have used this method have found it effective. Again it is probably most effective when used in conjunction with other methods, which take account of the problems of individuals.

Kounin's study

An American researcher, Kounin (1970), studied the techniques used by effective teachers. A good deal of his work was with young children, but much of it applies at later stages. He started by looking at the ripple effect of reproving an individual student. At high school level he found that the effectiveness of this on the behaviour of other students depended on their motivation for learning and their liking for the teacher. Highly motivated students who liked the teacher were more affected by comments made to another student about behaviour than those with low motivation who disliked the teacher.

He identified a number of teacher behaviours associated with high work involvement and low deviancy on the part of students. These were as follows.

- Withitness: the ability of the teacher to communicate to the students his or her awareness of what was happening in the classroom, the ability to target the right student for any reproof and to catch deviant behaviour at an early stage before it had time to escalate.
- Overlapping: the ability to maintain attention to one event while dealing with another.
- Smoothness: the ability to manage change from one activity to the next smoothly, without bursting in on the activities students are engaged in in an insensitive way or starting to terminate one activity and then going back to it.
- Slowdowns: avoiding anything which slows the pace of the lesson and maintaining pace towards the main objectives.

Reality therapy

Glasser (1969) devised a scheme called reality therapy to deal with students who posed problems. This involved:

- securing student involvement, which needs good relationships and honesty;
- identifying problem behaviour and making the student aware of this;
- evaluating inappropriate behaviour and asking the student to make judgements about this;
- gaining commitment from the student and making an oral or written plan;
- accepting no excuses, getting the student to re-evaluate when things went badly and re-commit himself or herself to the plan;
- avoiding punishment.

Teaching self-control

Gnagey (1975: 29) suggests the following.

- Describe the misbehaviour clearly so that the student knows exactly what he has been doing. Be sure he has just as clear a picture of what he should do instead.

- Ask the student to count the times he breaks the rule and note what happens just before and just after he misbehaves.
- Help the student to change the stimuli which come just before the mis-behaviour or punish himself immediately after he misbehaves.
- Ask the student to count and record the times he does the preferred action and reward himself immediately afterwards.
- By explaining the principles with many illustrations, help students learn this general sequence for other situations calling for self-control.

('he' and 'himself' as in original)

Punishment

Most schools will have various sanctions that teachers can use, and if a student does not respond to reprimand it may be necessary to use whatever punish-ment the school makes available. This has a ripple effect on other students. It is important to be seen to be fair in punishing students and not to punish harshly.

There should be a warning before a punishment is given, but if the student is warned that repetition of behaviour will result in punishment, then it is important to punish if the behaviour is repeated. It should be made quite clear why the student is being punished.

However, there are problems about using punishment too freely, and the ideal is to try to manage without it as much as possible. Its effects tend to be short term. This is evident in that it tends to be the same students who are punished again and again. It may be damaging to the relationship the teacher is trying to build up with the student, though this is less likely if the student agrees that he or she was in the wrong. It also tends to draw attention to bad behaviour rather than good behaviour. In particular, students very much resent it when a whole class is punished, and this should be avoided.

Fontana (1994: 69) suggests that teachers should examine the effect of repri-mands and punishments. 'Without such examination, teachers may not only be inadvertently offering rewards when they imagine they are offering punish-ments, but may fail to see the potential punitive impact that certain actions available to them might actually have.' His point is that for some students any attention is better than none, and punishment may in fact make some into heroes in the eyes of their contemporaries.

Rewards

Research suggests that teachers do not make very much use of rewards for good behaviour. They praise good work and sometimes praise effort, though not as much as they might do, but rarely praise good behaviour. It is worth thinking about how you reward students for work, effort and behaviour. There may be a school system of rewards as well as sanctions, but if there is not, you need to set up a system of your own.

Rewards ideally come from the satisfaction of work well done, and you need to encourage students to seek rewards of this kind by helping them to reflect on their successes and achievements. They also come from external sources, such as praise, good marks and the approval of teachers and peers. The teacher's words of praise are important in helping young people to develop self-esteem. You need to ask yourself whether there are some students who rarely get positive comment. There is some evidence that teachers, not very surprisingly, give more praise to high achieving pupils and that boys receive more praise than girls. You need to be aware of this tendency and see that pupils who need praise get their fair share. From this point of view, it is a good idea if you can manage it to record some of the comments you write on students' work. This will alert you to any students who need a more positive approach, even if you have to look hard for something good to say. Displaying students' work is another way of showing that you value it and consider it worthy of publication.

One of the most effective rewards is a letter to parents when students have done really well, not only in actually achieving but in the effort they have made in work or behaviour. You will need to clear this with the school if you want to use it as a reward.

Fontana (1994: 78) suggests that the 'effectiveness of non-material rewards depends closely upon the *prestige* and *status* in which the person giving the rewards is held. If a teacher is liked and admired by the class, then generally individuals will value his or her praise and encouragement.'

PARTICULAR PROBLEMS OF BEHAVIOUR

Whole group appears to be creating problems

Where this happens the teacher needs to analyse the various reasons why it may be happening. Is your behaviour as teacher to blame? Are you demonstrating anger, scorn, threat or other behaviour in a way which irritates the students? Is it the particular task that is unsuitable for some students? Is the time of day contributing? What about the seating arrangements: are the trouble makers all sitting together and stirring up other people? Was the pace of the lesson too slow? Was a change of activity badly organized? Are you failing to scan the class so that some students feel they can get away with misbehaviour? Has the group just come from a lesson where the teacher has been very strict with them?

You need to make this analysis quickly, so that you can decide on a course of action that gives you control again. Stand where you can see all the students and ask for attention. If you have established a signal for when you want to speak to the whole class at an early stage of working with them, you will be able to use it on this kind of occasion. Pick out by name those students who are ready and doing the right thing. Make eye contact with those who are doing the wrong thing and gesture them to sit down and attend. When you have sufficient attention, what you do next will depend upon the cause of the loss of control. If what went wrong was a badly organized change of activity

Case study 7

Jeremy found his first year of teaching mathematics tough going. His lessons started off all right but seemed to get out of hand as time went on. He asked his mentor to observe a lesson and see if he could identify what was going wrong.

His mentor noted a lot of small things. Jeremy did not organize things like giving out books and materials. As he quite often wrote on the board while this was going on, books were thrown across the classroom and Jeremy did nothing about this because he was not observing what was happening.

When there was a change of activity things tended to go wrong, because the organization had not been thought out. In particular, the room became chaotic when the students were asked to get into groups. His mentor suggested that he should start with groups which did not require much moving about the room. He should be very clear what everyone was to do and he should make sure that no one moved until he had given all the instructions.

He also allowed himself to become involved with individual students, without watching what was happening in the rest of the class.

Jeremy discussed his organization in detail with his mentor and found that things went a lot better when he prepared these aspects more carefully. He also tried hard to keep scanning the class so that problems were nipped in the bud. It took some time before he was able to get through a whole lesson with everything going well, but he gradually made progress.

then try again, breaking down the organization into small steps and getting students to do one thing at a time. If the problem was more one of students not concentrating on the work they were given, perhaps because it was too easy or too difficult, it may be a good idea to change the activity under way for one which demands immediate concentration. For example, you might give a short written test with a series of questions about the work the class has been doing, making it clear that the test will be marked. Move towards any student who appears to be about to disrupt proceedings, reminding him or her that the test is important.

When the lesson is over, try to analyse in more detail what went wrong and think out how you can avoid a similar situation on another occasion.

Apathy

Lambley (1993) makes the following points about pupils who are apathetic and not motivated to learn:

Pupils who lack success in learning often react to failure by non-involvement strategies. Their withdrawal of effort can show in various forms: total lack of motivation and retreat into dullness and laziness, avoidance strategies (such as distraction, fidgeting, day-dreaming) or resistance to the learning task expressed in such action as antagonistic and aggressive behaviour.

(Lambley 1993: 86)

She suggests that part of the problem is that young people develop their own expectations about their future performance, and some, partly because of home influence, see what happens to them as outside their control:

A person with an internal locus of control perceives success or failure as a consequence of his or her own action. In the case of a person with an external locus of control, outcomes appear unrelated to the individual's action and beyond his or her control. Success or failure are attributed to, for example, luck, fate, chance, parents or the teacher.

(Lambley 1993 : 87)

This is a long-term problem, which involves demonstrating to the pupil over and over again that he or she can succeed and that you believe in his or her ability. Matching work to such pupils is important, but because they are prepared to make very little effort, it is easy to underestimate what they can do if they try.

Hamblin (1978: 72) suggests that much can be done during the pastoral care period to promote attitude change:

The most effective step to tackle attitude change is to create conditions within the pastoral period under which pupils can examine the costs and utility of their attitudes, look at alternatives and select a new way of tackling study within the context of a supportive group of peers and through activities and experiences.

It may be worth your while discussing the problem with the form tutor. You may also find it helpful to discuss the problem with the student. This involves finding out how the student views himself or herself and the environment of school and home, working to change attitudes and trying to help the student to see that he or she is able to control what happens to a considerable degree. Such students need to be led to recognize that in the present climate young people who leave school with very poor qualifications are likely to have difficulty in finding work.

Dealing with confrontation

You may at some time be confronted by a pupil who refuses to do as asked, perhaps swears at you or generally acts in a confrontational manner. The rest of the class will be watching breathlessly to see what happens, and your method of dealing with the problem has a substantial ripple effect.

If you have students in the group who are likely to pose this kind of problem you should, in the first instance, try to avoid a situation in which a student is prepared to act in this way. Kyriacou (1986) suggests that the following teacher behaviours lead to confrontation:

- physical or verbal intimidation by the teacher;
- public embarrassment of the student or attempting to make a student lose face in front of the class;
- losing one's temper with a student;
- behaving in a way the student finds irritating.

You are in a position to avoid all but the last of these situations. However, such behaviour may well stem from the student's experience in the previous class, from home difficulties or from frustration with the work he or she is being asked to do.

When this kind of situation occurs you usually have little time to think. If confrontation happens it is important to appear to keep calm. Even though you may be boiling inside, you need to act in a calm way, using a calm and relaxed tone of voice. The student may have difficulty in scaling down his or her reaction once involved in confrontation so you need to look for an escape route for you both and try to defuse the situation. You need to be as non-threatening as possible. You can then take one of several courses of action.

You can separate the student from the others. You may do this in various ways. You can perhaps take him or her out of the room or at least out of earshot, if not out of sight, of other students, in order to talk without an audience, saying something like 'Let's go and talk this over.' When you get outside, start the conversation by asking what the problem was about. Talk in a quiet and friendly way and sound sympathetic rather than indignant. This is probably the best solution and has the advantage of ending the drama. How you deal with the student then will depend upon the particular student and the situation, but you have a better chance of making an impression when the student is not playing to the gallery. Once the student comes back into the class you should deal with him or her exactly as you would any other student, possibly looking at work and making comments or suggestions in a positive way. Some schools have a time-out room where students posing serious problems in the classroom can be sent and which are under the supervision of a senior member of staff. This is not intended as a punishment, but as an opportunity to cool off.

You can assert your authority. You can do this in any way you think may be effective. Some teachers demonstrate blank astonishment that anyone could do such a thing; others produce a show of anger, looking directly at the student and maintaining eye contact while moving towards him or her. Both of these can work, but you have to feel reasonably confident that this kind of action will not lead to further defiance. It is also easier to stay in control of the situation if you are acting as if you are astonished or angry and not really feeling it. This is often difficult to do, and this approach is generally rather risky because it threatens the self-esteem of the student who is already very sensitive about it.

You can pass it off lightly. You can imply that it is not important by saying something like 'I'm sure you didn't really mean that. How about starting again?' Then you take a later opportunity to talk to the student in question and try to find out what caused the outburst.

You can behave as if nothing has happened. You can more or less ignore the behaviour at the time and discuss it later. If you are dealing with a student whose behaviour is known to be abnormal and recognized by the other students to be so, this is not an unreasonable thing to do, especially if you can couple it with an opportunity to retract or rephrase what was said. A comment like 'I didn't quite hear that. Would you mind repeating it?' frequently produces something more moderate.

You can ignore the behaviour and concentrate on the student's work. This might involve acting as if he or she has asked for help or finding something good to say about what has been done. This again is something to do if the student is recognized by other students to be somewhat abnormal.

Get help if you feel that the situation may get out of hand. Find out which of your colleagues will be prepared to help if a situation gets out of hand, and be ready to make use of that help. It is not an admission of failure as a teacher to admit that sometimes things get too much for you. It is also important to remember that occasional failure is a means of learning. Try to think out why the situation happened and how you might have dealt with it differently at the early stages.

Gray and Richer (1988: 51) stress that interventions of whatever kind are intended to prevent escalation of the situation and get the class back to work. They make the following points about disruptive behaviour:

- Behaviour that leads to disruption arises essentially from the insecurity of the pupil.
- A prime source of that insecurity is frustration, especially that stemming from a mismatch between the external expectations made of the pupil and his [sic] internal self-evaluation.
- The two prime areas for such mismatch are the task and the social dimensions that make up the predominant agenda of the classroom.

It may be useful to keep a note of the situations where a student has been particularly difficult, noting what led up to the situation. If you do this over a period, you may be able to see a pattern in what triggers unacceptable behaviour, and this might enable you to avoid situations which create problems or discuss them with the student in question, to see if he or she can overcome the problem.

All confrontation issues are better dealt with after a cooling off period and away from an audience. If you are counselling at the end of a lesson or later you should try to show a caring and concerned attitude and try to discover what triggered off the display on the part of the student. It may be a good idea to talk about how you felt about it. Encourage the student to evaluate his or her own behaviour and if possible get him or her to agree to try to behave in a more moderate way.

In some situations you may have to deal with defence mechanisms; for example, denial and rationalization. If possible, explain to the student that he or she is using defence mechanisms and try to get him or her to see things from someone else's point of view.

In the end, if it is a matter of a student refusing to do something (for example, refusing to move to another seat because he or she is misbehaving in the present place and not prepared to leave the room to discuss it with you), you may need to involve a more senior colleague in removing the student from the class.

BODY LANGUAGE

Sotto (1994: 150) notes that 'The way teachers communicate in a lesson surely conveys much more than facts or ideas. It conveys the kind of people they are and how they feel about other people. It also conveys the kind of attitude toward learning and teaching they have and the kind of values they hold.' There is a great deal of communication by body language in most classrooms on the part of both students and teachers. Neill and Caswell (1993: 9) note that 'Non-verbal communication includes face-to-face interaction, actual behaviour and signals, such as dress and room arrangement which you or the children may "set up" before you meet each other, also facial expression, gaze, head and body posture, hand movements, interpersonal distance and spacing, intonation and pace of speech.'

The teacher's body language

Your body language and the way you use verbal communication tells the students a great deal and it helps if you are aware of some of the ways in which you communicate. Kyriacou (1986: 6) makes the following point about the teacher's language:

> The teacher's language conveys – through the types of phrases used, its tone, and how and when it is used – a whole range of messages to pupils about the teacher's perceptions and expectations regarding learning and teaching. What is now apparent is that pupils pick up such messages with great sophistication and often with consequences that the teacher may be unaware of and not intend.

Cohen and Manion (1983: 231) make a similar point: 'If children detect discrepancies between what a teacher says and what he actually does, they will ignore what he says and be affected much more by what he does. Further if they see discrepancies between what he says, he expects, and what he allows, they will tend to be influenced by what he allows.'

In a later edition of the same book, Cohen and Manion (1989: 255) say: 'The teacher's tone of voice is of considerable importance in establishing emotional tone in a classroom. If it is relaxed, natural and mainly conversational in tone it will assist in creating a relaxed, tension-free atmosphere favourable to interaction and learning.' It is useful to remember that a quiet voice and a lower pitch tend to be more effective than a loud, high-pitched voice. Any teacher who has had to teach after having lost his or her voice will know that this leads to the whole class tending to whisper.

Students need to know that you like them. This is communicated by being ready to look at them and be near them, listening attentively and nodding when they tell you something. Smiling helps to create a relaxed atmosphere and also shows that you like them. 'Shouting, staring, frowning and keeping at a distance from the pupil all tend to be seen as signals that the pupil is disliked. It is threatening for a pupil to feel disliked and that generates great anxiety' (Gray and Richer 1988: 55).

Human beings in different cultures tend to keep a certain distance apart. The accepted distance varies from one culture to another, and if you move closer than the accepted distance it intensifies whatever you are communicating. If you move closer to a student in order to offer praise, the praise will be more appreciated. If you move closer in order to call a student to order, that student will find the movement threatening and the comment may be more effective. Neill and Caswell (1993: 81) suggest that a forward leaning posture 'communicates greater involvement . . . you will appear more friendly, more interested in your subject or more forcefully in control.'

They also have some valuable things to say about dominance and threat:

Dominance is the ability to control or influence the behaviour of others. *Threat* is behaviour which indicates that there is a risk of physical attack (i.e. an escalated confrontation) unless the opponent gives way. Dominance does *not* imply confrontation; in fact if dominance is well established, the subordinate will give way without any confrontation. Threat indicates that dominance is not fully established, and the more extreme the threat, the greater the risk to dominance.

(Neill and Caswell 1993: 129)

You can also use a form of distancing to dominate a situation. If you are standing and the student is sitting you are in the dominant position. If you want to create a more equal situation, you may crouch beside a student who is sitting or bring him or her to sit beside you at your desk. There are other positions that indicate domination, such as a raised chin.

Most people gesture as they talk. Hand gestures reinforce what you are saying and the listener needs to watch as well as listen. 'Lack of gestures indicates lack of involvement with and mastery of the ideas being communicated and thus gives a clear signal to the class that you are not on top of your subject' (Neill and Caswell 1993: 117).

The students' body language

You not only need to be aware of your own body language, you also need to be able to read the students' body language. The important thing is to be able to recognize body language which indicates that serious misbehaviour is starting. Students about to do something disruptive will give quick glances at you to see if you are looking before they act. They may look round the class to find potential allies, and other students may be distracted from their work by this. The noise level may increase. If you can recognize these signs and move towards the students who are involved, reminding them to get on with their work, you may succeed in preventing problems from arising.

Brown (1975) suggests looking for the following signals in monitoring the class.

- Posture: are students turned towards or away from the object of the lesson?
- Head orientation: are students looking at or away from the object of the lesson?
- Faces: do students look sleepy or awake? Do they look withdrawn or involved? Interested or uninterested?
- Activities: are they working on something related to the lesson or are they attending to something else? Where they are talking to their fellow students are their discussions task-oriented?

Neill and Caswell (1993: 59) suggest that students about to challenge you show variation in posture:

> Often they will be seen with head low on the desk, sometimes shielded by an arm, bag or the back of the pupil in front. They often sit much lower than usual in their seats. Both these postures conceal their actions from you. Alternatively they may be perched on the edge of the chair, poised to change position in the event of your unwanted attention.

It is important not to be misled by the expressions on students' faces. Students may look as if they are understanding when they are not or, conversely, may develop a puzzled look when they are not really puzzled. The absorbed look may hide day dreaming about something quite different from the content of the lesson.

ENDING THE LESSON

Keep careful track of time, so that you end the lesson in time to give homework and to do any clearing up necessary, and so that you leave the room ready for the next class. Allow a little time to talk to the students about what they have learned during the lesson. This might take the form of questioning, a short pencil and paper test or simply discussion. Summarize the important points, so that you send students away with a clear idea of what they should have learned. Leave enough time to set homework and answer any questions about it. It is better to have time to spare than to be overtaken by the bell. If your school does not use bells to end periods, it is particularly important to end your lesson on time.

If there is still some time left after you have dealt with the end of lesson suggestions above, be ready with a filler activity. This might be talking to the students or questioning them about the work they have been doing or the work they will be doing in the next lesson or lessons, adding to their knowledge of the topic they have been studying, playing a relevant game designed to reinforce some particular learning or any other idea you may have.

Schools and individual teachers have different processes for ending lessons. Some simply allow students to pack up and walk out quietly. Others insist that students go out a row at a time or a table at a time. The more adult approach is to get students walking out quietly and this means getting them quiet before they leave the lesson.

Checklist 7 – Classroom management

- Is my preparation adequate?
- Am I managing the beginning of lessons adequately?
- How well am I managing changes of activity?
- Have I given students clear information about the rules of the classroom?
- Am I doing sufficient to establish them?
- Do I convey confidence in the classroom?
- How well am I dealing with misbehaviour?
- Am I using praise sufficiently, for behaviour as well as good work and effort?
- Am I learning to read students' body language?
- Am I ending lessons effectively?

AFTER THE LESSON

Try to find time to review what happened in at least some lessons each day. Ask yourself how much learning took place – the work students did will give you some clues about this. Did the lesson start well? How satisfactory was your organization? Did changes of activity go smoothly? Were there any behaviour problems? Are you happy with the way you dealt with them, or do you think you might have done better to have acted differently? What was the context of such problems? Could you have avoided them if you had planned differently? Were there some students who did not benefit from the work you did?

How could you deal differently with them on another occasion? Was the balance of time about right? Did you start to conclude the lesson in time? Did the lesson ending go smoothly? Did you achieve your objectives?

Earley and Kinder (1995: 38) say that 'Once you are a reflective practitioner you never let it go. Reflective practitioners have better stress levels, they see the classroom as a set of inter-connected events, they are part of it, they can manipulate events and do it for professional reasons – that removes the emotion from the situation.'

FURTHER READING

Charlton, T. and David, K. (eds) (1993) *Managing Misbehaviour in School*, 2nd edn. London: Routledge. Looks at causes of misbehaviour and ways in which teachers can tackle it.

Department of Education and Science and Welsh Office (1989) *Discipline in Schools: Report of the Committee of Enquiry Chaired by Lord Elton*. London: HMSO. The official report on discipline which contains much useful material.

Fontana, D. (1985) *Managing Classroom Behaviour*. Leicester: British Psychological Society. Looks at many of the aspects of schooling which affect students' self-esteem and the effect of low self-esteem on behaviour.

Gnagey, W. (1975) *Maintaining Discipline in Classroom Instruction*. London: Collier Macmillan. A brief but useful survey of some of the issues which affect control in the classroom.

Gray, J. and Richer, J. (1988) *Classroom Responses to Disruptive Behaviour*. London: Macmillan Education. Describes research into disruptive incidents in schools and disruptive students and draws some useful conclusions from this.

Kounin, J. (1970) *Discipline and Group Management in Classrooms*. New York: Holt, Rinehart and Winston. An interesting account of a study of discipline which makes useful suggestions.

Lawrence, J., Steed, D. and Young, P. (1984) *Disruptive Children, Disruptive Schools*. London: Routledge. Suggests a need to be analytical in dealing with cases of disruption and to avoid labelling students as disruptive.

Neill, S. and Caswell, C. (1993) *Body Language for Competent Teachers*. London: Routledge. A comprehensive and valuable account of the use of body language in the classroom.

Wheldall, K. and Merrett, F. (1984) *Positive Teaching: the Behavioural Approach*. London: Unwin Educational Books. A clear account of behaviour modification which gives many useful pointers to teachers.

7

THE MANAGEMENT OF TIME AND SPACE

Organization of work in the classroom is not only a matter of organizing the students and the learning material. It also involves organizing the use of time and space.

THE USE OF TIME

Time once spent cannot be recovered. We can only try to make better use of it. We may appear to be working hard but unless the hard work results in effective learning on the part of students our time and their time is not being well used. Using time well is self-fulfilling, helps to avoid stress and gives time for leisure pursuits. Fontana (1993: 11) suggests that 'Good time managers are people who are able not only to meet all reasonable demands upon their time, but are able to do so without draining away too much of their physical and psychological resources.' You need to study yourself and your particular problems with time.

There has not been a great deal of study of the use of time in schools compared with studies of industry. An American study, *Time to Learn* (Denham and Leiberman 1980), found, not very surprisingly, that there was a high correlation between *engaged student time* and *achievement*. It also found that high achievement went with high success and that the student who frequently needed and obtained extra help still achieved less. The study implied that the teacher might get the slower students to achieve more and use time more effectively by doing more to anticipate their needs. Such students needed work in which they could succeed by taking a series of small steps, which were demanding for them but which they could take without help. This approach might be more effective than responding to requests for help, which implied that the student had already realized that he or she was failing.

What can be learned from this study is that the best teaching occurs when the teacher is able to match individual learning in such a way that all students have work which challenges, but at which they can succeed. However, this is an ideal state that teachers can aim for, but you should not feel too despondent if you cannot achieve it.

Using time well: aims and objectives

Moon (1985), Adair (1987) and Fontana (1993) offer general advice on the use of time. Moon and Adair write for industrial managers and Fontana writes for anyone who wants to use time more effectively, but much of their advice applies to schools. They suggest that to use time well you need to:

- have clear long-term aims;
- have medium- and short-term goals which are clearly stated in specific terms;
- have clear priorities;
- know how your time is actually spent;
- know your own best use of time;
- plan time for evaluation, reflection and planning;
- plan time for contingencies;
- plan time for relaxation;
- have sufficient self-discipline to manage your time.

If you are to use time well you need a clear picture of where you want to go in life, in personal and in professional terms and both short term and long term. You then need aims and goals for your work year by year, month by month, week by week and today. Your short-term goals need to have some relation to your long-term goals, but they will reflect current demands on your time. Your long-term goals may be part of the plan you made in the context of appraisal.

Aims can be stated in broad terms and may reflect philosophy. For example, one aim of all your teaching might be to stimulate enthusiasm for your subject in the students you teach. Goals are much more specific and are really behavioural objectives, and should therefore be stated in terms that can be assessed. For example, an aim for your first month in a new post might be getting to know names. As a goal it needs to be stated in precise terms, such as 'get to know the names of my own form and of students I teach in year 7'. This enables you to judge whether you have achieved this goal, whereas a vague 'get to know students' names' cannot really be assessed. In terms of time management you need goals like 'mark year 7's work the day it is given in', or whatever seems to be a possible goal that you can actually achieve. Fontana (1993: 14) suggests giving yourself 'a few small realistic time-management targets each day'.

Most people have an inaccurate idea of how they are spending their time. How you use your teaching time depends a good deal on your particular style of teaching, but it is very easy to think you are using time in one way and to find when you analyse it that this is not really the case. It is necessary to keep a time log for three or four fairly typical days to get a clear idea of how your time is being spent. It would be very difficult, though extremely valuable, to do this for your time in the classroom, but it is much easier to do it for your time out-of-class. To do this you need to decide on a number of headings under which different activities can be listed. For example, you might list your out-of-class activities under the following headings: preparation, marking, talking to students, talking with colleagues, extra-curricular activity, meetings, courses, professional reading, leisure activities, other. These can then be analysed in terms of how far you are using time to achieve the goals and priorities you have set yourself.

When you have completed your time logs for two or three days, add up how you are using time under the various headings and work out the percentages of time you have used on different activities. Consider these against your goals for your work and consider whether you are happy with the way you are actually using time or whether it should be changed in any way.

There may be things that you are doing which you could do more efficiently or not do at all without loss. You also need to consider whether the items on your time log are contributing to long- or short-term goals.

Body rhythms

Each individual has a body rhythm, which determines how he or she feels at different times of the day. Most people feel freshest in the morning but some people work well late at night; others find the early evening or the early morning a good time for work. People also vary in whether they work best in short spells or need a long clear period to settle down to a major piece of work. Consider your own body rhythm, and try to make use of this knowledge. You have no choice about your use of time in the classroom, but you can decide when best to do work out-of-school.

Teachers should spend time evaluating, reflecting and planning, but it is easy when under pressure to regard time spent on these activities as a low priority, particularly time spent on planning the use of time. These activities are in fact essential to managing time well and being an effective teacher, and need to be planned into your programme. Plans for using your time should be written down, so that you feel a commitment to them. Time spent in planning the use of time should result in time saved. You also need to assess the effectiveness of your time plans after the event.

Sometimes your planning is interrupted by contingencies. You plan the work you will do in a free period and then find that it is taken up by covering for an absent colleague. If you keep account over several weeks of the time taken by this sort of thing you may find that there is a certain regularity about the amount of time used up by unexpected things. You can then plan contingency time into your programme, knowing that if it is not used it will not be difficult to find other work to do. You will, of course, not know when the contingencies are going to arise, so you will need to do some rearrangements when they do occur, but you will still be in a position to complete the work you planned.

It is very easy to find yourself spending all your time on work. This is not a good idea. If you are to avoid a damaging amount of stress, it is essential that you have some time for relaxation and for activities other than work, and good planning should allow for this.

Time management requires the self-discipline to make plans and keep to them: to keep goals in mind and work towards them.

Some ways of managing time well

The following ideas may be helpful in using time well:

- from your time analysis identify practices that are losing time for you;
- have a daily 'to do' list;
- split up large tasks so that you can do a bit at a time;
- use short periods of time;
- change tasks when you become bored;
- see if there are any tasks you can delegate to students;
- recognize whether you have a tendency to procrastinate;
- have routines and systems for dealing with things both at home and at school;
- try to do something with each piece of paper which comes to you, rather than putting it on a pile;
- develop a good filing system;
- keep your desk clear;
- learn to say 'no' pleasantly to requests from both inside and outside the school which do not fit into your planning.

There are many things that lose time. Mislaying things is one. You are less likely to do this if you have a place for everything and are self-disciplined about returning things to their places after using them. Worrying about something that has happened or is going to happen is another. Give time to thinking what you can learn from something that has happened and to planning to meet your worries about the future, and then do your utmost to concentrate on something else. This is not easy, but you can improve with practice. You may also be inclined to spend longer chatting than is profitable, or you may procrastinate over starting tasks that you do not much like. Try to identify ways in which you can avoid falling into these traps, and give yourself targets in appropriate cases to avoid them.

You need to list in order to keep in mind the various jobs you have to do, so that you can prioritize them and check them off as you do them. Check over your list each morning or the evening before, noting which items are priorities for the following day. You can do this by marking items A, B or C according to their priority, or simply highlighting those you intend to put first. Fontana (1993) suggests that there are three kinds of priority: priority of time, priority of importance and priority of time and importance. Clearly the third group needs to be dealt with first, and then priorities of time. It is useful to set a time limit for items on your list.

If you have a large task or a task you don't much want to do, it is tempting to put off doing it until you can give it a long spell of time, which may mean putting it off almost indefinitely. A better approach with a large task is to split it up in some way so that you can do parts of it in short spells of time. Tasks you don't much want to do should be given a certain amount of priority so that you get them out of the way.

Sometimes you have only a short period of time available. Organize yourself so that you use that time. There are many things that can be done in ten minutes and the short periods of time add up. If you become bored with a task, change tasks for a period. When you are flogging yourself to do something your work is likely to deteriorate, and it is better to motivate yourself by working at something different.

See if there are any tasks you do which you could delegate to students. For example, marking work is a major task for secondary school teachers. Occasionally you might try getting students to work in pairs, marking each other's work using a set of criteria you have discussed with them. This is good for them, because it makes them conscious of the criteria by which you are judging work, and it relieves your burden a little. There may be other ways in which students can contribute. For example, it has already been suggested that a group having studied a particular area of work might be asked to work in groups to make worksheets that could be used by another group. They would need to study the groups for whom the worksheets were being made, and it should be specified whether the sheets are for very able or less able students. They will also need help in thinking about layout and language. The worksheets may not be usable in the form in which the students have left them, but they will have quite a bit of usable material and this is an interesting way of testing knowledge and the ability to write for other people. Students will be able to undertake many routine tasks in the classroom, like keeping materials in order and checking that things have been returned.

Note the things that happen to interrupt your plans. Can any of them be avoided by more careful planning or by a different organization? With year 7 students in particular there will be occasions when they check with you that they are doing the right thing or that they can take some particular action. The clearer you are about what you want, the fewer these interruptions will become. The rules you make for work in the classroom should take care of a number of queries.

Most of us have a tendency to waste time. We put off doing things. We find something interesting on television. We chat when we might have been working. Up to a point this is natural and probably useful in relieving tension, but if you do it too much you do not do things which are important for your teaching. One way of avoiding some of this is to have routines for doing things and to stick to them. For example, getting everything ready for the morning before you go to bed is a useful habit which saves you worry next day, especially if you are a person who finds getting up difficult.

Most teachers and others find that there is a continual battle to keep on top of the paper that arrives, both at home and at work. Try to make it a rule to do something positive with each piece of paper. Throw away the junk mail as soon as you have decided it is not of interest. If it is of interest deal with it or file it as quickly as possible. Pass on to someone else anything that might be of use to them. Reply to memos by writing on them and sending them back. Have a day in the week when you go through what remains and deal with it. Develop a good filing system for correspondence and for resource materials and overhead projector transparencies, and allow time to file as you go.

Try to keep your desk top clear, except for material you are currently using. Clear it each night before you go home. Even if you simply put things in drawers and close them, it still gives you a more business-like space for work on the next day.

In your early days in teaching you will be asked to undertake many activities in addition to teaching. Some of these may be really valuable to you in terms of your skill development, and you will want to use the opportunities offered. Others may be less valuable, and you need to be able to say 'no' pleasantly when this is the case and when additional work would make problems for your use of time. It is a good idea when saying 'no' to give a reason why. It is likely in your first year of teaching that you cannot fit any more into your time without becoming overstretched, and people should be able to understand this. Try not to be tempted to take on something extra because it is attractive to you.

Managing time in the classroom

The aim of every teacher must be to use the time available with students to the best possible effect. In practice, research suggests that a good deal of time is spent in classroom routines and administration compared with the proportion of time spent in learning activities. The teacher's task is to try to increase the time spent in learning. The following points may be helpful.

- Ensure that students use the time while you are waiting for a class to assemble for learning. It has already been suggested that, if you work in a school where students come straight into the classroom as soon as they arrive, you have a small but interesting task on the overhead projector for them to do while they are waiting for the rest of the class. Over a period one can make a collection of these. Alternatively, you may train them to do a particular task, such as looking over the previous lesson's work, while they are waiting.

- Keep a note of occasions when little learning is going on. Note down after or during a lesson those occasions when learning seems limited, and try to analyse why and what could be done to avoid such occasions in future.
- Have procedures for all the routines of the classroom. It saves time if everyone knows what should be done in getting things out and clearing up, for example. You need routines for when you wish to move students into groups, for beginning and ending lessons and for many other regular activities.
- Look for occasions when students are held up because they are waiting for help from you. If there are too many of these you may be pitching the work at the wrong level. If the students waiting for your attention are always the less able, then perhaps you need to provide work for them that is rather easier. It may be a good idea to encourage students to help each other and ask you only when they are unable to get help from a colleague. It is sometimes helpful to discuss the problem with students to see whether they felt the work was wrongly pitched and whether they have solutions to the problem of waiting for your attention.
- Discuss the whole issue of increasing learning time with students. See what ideas they have for ensuring that time is used fully. They may be able to identify times when learning could be increased of which you are not really aware.
- Consider whether your teaching strategies are leading to optimum learning. Students may be able to help you by discussing which teaching strategies they feel they get most from. For example, we have already noted that research suggests that lecturing is effective for short periods only. People make learning their own only when they actually use what they have learned.
- Train students in the necessary study skills. The better your students are as independent learners, the more effectively they will use the time available. Learning to study is an ongoing process at which you need to work regularly, dealing with issues like effective reading, organizing written work, evaluating one's work and so on.
- Involve students in managing their time. Much of the material in this chapter can be used with students. In particular, it is valuable for them to do some analysis of the way their time is being used. In Chapter 6 it was suggested that using a timer and recording how many students are on task is a good way of getting students to increase the time on task. It can also be used to get students to assess what they are doing when the timer goes. This sort of analysis helps to make students conscious of the need to use time profitably in class.

Starting to manage time

When all the aspects of managing time are put together they sound somewhat intimidating. As with any large task, the thing to do is to undertake a little at a time. You will probably already have done some work on defining objectives as part of your normal work. The next thing to concentrate on is finding out how you are actually using time and starting a daily 'to do' list if you don't do this already. You can then select out of the various things you have identified one or two aspects of time management to start trying to implement. Build on these, gradually dealing with new areas.

It is a good idea to reflect on how you use the time in lessons and to compare the time you actually use for different activities with the time stated in your lesson plans. This will help you to become better at estimating how long different activities will take.

If you get depressed about the pressure of time, remember that you are doing everything for the first time this year. Next year will be easier, especially if you file your notes and materials carefully. You will want to adapt them and change them in the light of this year's experience, but they will give you a starting point that you lack this year.

Learning to manage time well is not easy. It takes self-discipline and needs to be worked at over a period. It does not become easier overnight, but is a long-term commitment.

Checklist 8 – Time management

- Have I long- and short-term aims and objectives?
- Do I prioritize the use of my time?
- Do I know how my time is actually spent?
- What time of day is the best working time for me?
- Do I plan the use of my time?
- Do I allow for contingencies?
- Do I allow time for relaxation and activities other than school work?
- Have I a daily 'to do' list?
- Do I check this each day?
- Do I use short periods of time efficiently?
- Have I routines for dealing with chores?
- Have I a good filing system?
- Is my desk normally clear at the end of the day?
- Do I use time effectively in the classroom?
- Are there times when learning is not taking place?
- Do I do anything to help students manage their time?

THE USE OF SPACE

Organizing a learning environment

You may be one of the less fortunate teachers in the school who needs to have lessons in a variety of rooms, none of which is your own base. If you do not have the benefit of a permanent classroom in which most of your teaching takes place, you need to have your books and materials very well organized and you can do little to use display as a stimulus for your students, although you may be able to persuade a colleague to spare you a little space in a room you use fairly frequently. If you have to wander for most of your work it pays to have something like a large plastic container in which you can put most of the books and materials you need.

If, however, you have a base room, the organization of this is important for your teaching. It needs to be functional. This involves:

- an arrangement of furniture which provides the optimum conditions for the work to be done;
- an organization of books and materials which shows clearly what is available and is arranged so that it can be used by students without difficulty and without a great deal of attention from the teacher;
- an organization in which it is easy to keep materials and equipment clean, tidy and in order, and that is easy to check over to see that everything is in the right place;
- a discriminating use of display which provides standards to aim for, so that your room reflects a view of your subject.

Having your own room enables you to organize seating and resources to suit your teaching. The way you organize seating depends upon the way you work for the majority of the time. If you teach mainly by talking to the whole class, then questioning them, followed by individual work, it makes sense to have traditional seating with desks all facing the front. If you want a lot of discussion, it is better to arrange desks or tables in a horseshoe, so that students can see each other. This makes for better discussion. If much of your work is in groups, then you may prefer to seat students in groups, though this poses problems when you want to work with the whole class and students need to turn their chairs so that they are facing front. Waterhouse (1983) suggests that there is a case for seating students in groups round the periphery of the room and using the centre for resources. This makes it easy to bring everyone into a group in the middle of the room for discussion.

The extent to which you need different resources will differ from subject to subject, but if students need quite a number of resources for different work, you need to organize your resources on a self-service basis. This means having them set out so that they can easily be seen and so that each item has its own place. It pays to draw round each item with a felt pen on a paper shelf covering, which can then be labelled. This makes it easy to see that everything has been returned to its proper place at the end of a lesson. Items like scissors, which need to be counted back, are best placed in a block with the requisite number of spaces, but if you have to keep them in a box, the number there should be needs to be clearly written on the lid, so that a check can easily be made. Items like sticky tape are less likely to go missing if you attach them to a large piece of wood.

A permanent room makes it possible to use display. This creates an atmosphere relevant to the subject, and some part of it should be deliberately planned to interest students or to be used as part of your teaching. You may want to display reference material so that students can turn to it when they need to. A large part of your display should be contributed by students. This can be used to set standards, so that on occasion you display the best work only. On another occasion you may want to use display to encourage students, particularly the less able. Sometimes you will want to set a standard of display and put it up yourself and sometimes you will want to train students in putting up display, perhaps making this the end product of a piece of work.

Checklist 9 – The use of space

- Have I the best possible arrangement of seating for the work I want to do?
- Are my resources well organized?
- Can students get what they need easily?
- Are resources returned to the right place easily?
- Do things disappear from my resource collection?
- Do I use display to interest students or as material for teaching? Do students actually look at what I have put up?
- When did I last change the display?
- Do I use display to create an atmosphere?
- Do I use display to set standards?
- Do I use display to encourage less able students?
- Do my students use display to show what they have learned?
- Are my students developing display skills?

FURTHER READING

Adair, J. (1987) *How to Manage Your Time*. Guildford: Talbot Adair/Mcgraw Hill. An account of time management written for industry, but suggesting many ideas which are relevant for schools.
Fontana, D. (1993) *Managing Time*. Leicester: British Psychological Society. Written with a fairly general readership in mind but containing much of value to schools. In

particular, there is a series of exercises leading to better time management, which could be valuable.

Moon, J. (1985) *A Time: the Busy Manager's Action Plan for Effective Self-management*. New York: Van Nostrand Reinhold (International). Also written for industry but relevant for schools.

Waterhouse, P. (1983) *Managing the Learning Process*. Maidenhead: McGraw-Hill. Has useful sections on the management of time and space.

8

STUDENTS WITH SPECIAL NEEDS

THE CODE OF PRACTICE ON THE IDENTIFICATION AND ASSESSMENT OF SPECIAL EDUCATION NEEDS

The code of practice was published in 1994 and sets out the way in which schools are to organize their work with students with special needs. It is clear from the code that all teachers are to be concerned with identification of such students and with teaching them at an appropriate level. At the school level there will be a coordinator, who will maintain a register of all students with special needs, will be responsible for the overall organization and coordination, will liaise with parents and external agencies and will support and advise colleagues.

The code states that there will be five stages for providing help to such students. At stage 1 the form tutor, in consultation with subject teachers, identifies students with special educational needs and the parents and the student are consulted. The special needs coordinator is informed and he or she registers the student as having special needs. Form tutors and subject teachers then work with the student in the normal classroom context, collecting relevant information and consulting the special needs coordinator. The student's progress is monitored and reviewed.

If the teachers involved with the student think it necessary, the student may move on to stage 2. At this stage any relevant information from outside the school is included and an individual education plan is drawn up, the student and the parents are consulted and the headteacher is informed. The student's progress is again monitored and reviewed.

Stage 3 involves specialists from outside the school, such as educational psychologists and specialist teachers. The student and the parents are again consulted and a further individual education plan is drawn up. The outside specialists are then involved with the teachers in the process of monitoring and reviewing progress.

If the student is still giving cause for concern, the case goes on to stage 4 and is referred to the LEA, where a decision is made as to whether to make a statutory assessment. This involves reports from the school, the educational psychologist, the health service and social services. These may result in a move to stage 5, where a formal statement is made with recommendations about how the student's education should proceed. There will then be an annual review involving all those concerned in making the statement.

THE STUDENTS

It is important to find out as much as you can about any students who have special needs, including those who are outstandingly able, before you start teaching them. You cannot start to differentiate work for them until you know something about them, and it is wise to find out what is known already so that you can build on this. Ask at an early stage for the names of special needs students in the classes you teach and for any information about their particular needs. It is valuable to know of students who have sight or hearing problems, so that you can be aware of their difficulties and whether they should be wearing glasses or hearing aids. It is helpful to know about students who have serious learning difficulties and anything that works successfully in helping them to learn. The special needs coordinator should be able to give you a good deal of this information, as well as being able to help you in finding ways of catering for such students.

Students with learning difficulties

In every class there will be students who need individual help with some of the work. Some secondary schools contain students who would formerly have been in special schools. These may have disabilities of various kinds, which may or may not include learning difficulties.

If you teach a mixed-ability class, or one that includes students with special needs or some very able students, you will need to provide differentiated work for different groups of students and some individuals. Even if the classes are setted there will be a range of ability within any individual group, and you need to take account of this.

In many schools special needs staff work with other teachers in the classroom to support students with special needs; this not only helps the students but should be of help to you in learning how to teach such students. Some students with disabilities may also be provided with ancillary help to support them; this also makes things rather easier for the subject teacher. The special needs department and senior staff in your subject department ought to be prepared to advise you on how best to cope with students with various kinds of problems. In using this advice you will learn not only how to deal with students with special needs but also a good deal about teaching all students.

You need to get to know as much as possible about the individual students you teach if you are to be able to match learning to their needs. There is, of course, a limit to how far this is possible when you have large numbers of different classes, but in each class you need to get to know names as soon as possible and identify those students who need extra help and those who are outstandingly able. Most of these will identify themselves at a fairly early stage, but there will be a few quiet students who do not come to your attention for quite a while.

Your first task is diagnostic. The code of practice for special needs sees the form teacher as the person who identifies those students who need to be placed on the school register of students with special needs, but the form teacher needs to be advised by subject teachers. You need to observe and make notes about those who need extra help in each class, so that you can plan with this in mind. Other teachers will tell you about some of these students and, while you may want to make up your own mind about them, it is only sensible to use any valid knowledge that other people have accumulated. It is very hard on a student who has reading difficulties to be asked by a new teacher to read aloud in class and an embarrassment that you would want to avoid, since it is damaging to your future relationships with that student.

You also need to differentiate for very able students. HMI, in its study of new teachers (DES: 1987: 14), makes the following points: 'All too frequently able pupils were not extended because the teacher had given insufficient thought to their needs. Where the needs of less able pupils were not catered for, teachers had not anticipated the need to set differentiated tasks.'

Students who have learning difficulties are at risk, whatever their age. They cannot afford to waste time. It is essential that they receive appropriate help as soon as possible. The school will almost certainly offer additional help to such students, perhaps by supporting them in normal classes or withdrawing them for additional help. Subject teachers may still have to provide for them in their classes, and this means that all teachers have to learn how best to teach them.

Brennan (1979) showed that such students frequently achieved at a much lower level than their ability suggested. The demands of the National Curriculum may have changed this to some extent, but there is still a tendency for teachers to show, usually without intending to, that they have low expectations of these students. This leads to a lack of confidence on the student's part, which is reinforced by each subsequent failure. The skill needed is to give such students work which is demanding for them but within their capacity, so that they succeed and gain confidence in their ability to learn. Fontana (1994: 15) makes the point that slow learners have a particular need for a teacher who is sympathetic to their difficulties and patient. He points out that 'children confronted with habitual failure will often defend their sense of self-esteem by putting all the blame upon the school and the teacher.'

If you look at this problem from a different angle, you might say that every class is made up of individuals. Some of these individuals will be at about the same level for some work and will be able to learn together for part of the time. Others, for various reasons, may need some individual provision.

The special needs department will have diagnosis as a major task, and you may be able to contribute to their diagnostic work by observing students with special needs within your classes and noticing some of the particular problems they seem to experience. Some of them, such as the student with a physical disability or a lack of English, are easy to identify and see the reasons for the problems; other problems, such as that of the student who is thirteen, but whose reading age is nine, are comparatively easy to identify, but it may be difficult to discover the reasons for the problem and still more difficult to know what to do about it. Yet other problems may pass unnoticed for a time, such as the student with an undiagnosed hearing problem. This is especially true where the student is quiet and well behaved.

Students with learning difficulty form a very varied group. There will be students of low ability who are likely to need a certain amount of special attention at every stage of schooling, and this needs to be accepted and planned for. There will be some students who are apparently of average or above average intelligence but who are not achieving at their proper level. There will be others who appear to have difficulties in one particular aspect of their work, while managing the rest quite well. There may be students with physical disabilities which create problems for their learning. There may also be students with problems that have not yet been diagnosed, except insofar as some of their school work seems to be well below average.

The extent of the special attention they will need will depend upon the class they are with. If they are in a class where the average ability is low, the work is likely to be nearer the needs of students with low ability. A student of near average ability may need individual help if he or she is with a group of high flyers. This makes it difficult to talk about students with low or high ability in the abstract. Although the terms are defined by national norms of ability, the extent to which the level of ability of a particular individual student affects the work of the class is a matter of the norms within it and the particular ways in which the student's ability differs from the norm.

Students with low ability are likely to be at an earlier stage of the National Curriculum than other students in the class, and you will need to reward their progress with praise and encouragement, so that they develop a positive self-image. You can also help to develop their self-image by giving them responsibility within the classroom.

It is the responsibility of every teacher to try to teach every student in the class, so you must do your utmost to provide for such students without neglecting others, which is not easy. It may be necessary to break down the work into smaller steps that these students can actually take. They need a great deal of repetition and you need to think of different ways of giving them any necessary practice. In some contexts games may be useful. There is a good deal of computer software which provides good practice material. You also need to give them more practical experiences than other students. It can be helpful to pair a student with learning difficulties with one who is just about managing and to get them to work together on a number of tasks.

Worksheets need to be well spaced out, and it can sometimes be helpful to use worksheets where the student writes the answer on the sheet. Material for students with low ability needs to be in simple language, with short sentences.

Students who are apparently of average or above average ability may have difficulty in reading and writing or in mathematics, and it may be helpful to tape some work for them as well as having it on paper. You may also need to be prepared to accept some work on tape from them. Such students may have difficulty in sequencing, both in terms of spelling and with ideas. They will find it difficult to remember things in sequence and will have a poor memory for tables and number bonds. They may find it difficult to follow instructions, and need to get into the habit of making notes about what is required. It can be helpful in both writing and mathematics to collect errors that such students make. It is often possible to recognize from the errors that a student is making that he or she has not acquired a particular rule of spelling, for example, or a

Case study 8

Linda and Julie were part of Stephanie's geography class, and both had considerable learning difficulties. They were very slow to understand any new work, and Stephanie found that she spent a good deal of time explaining things to them after she had already explained them to the rest of the class.

She decided that the best thing to do would be to make special worksheets in advance for them, making them rather carefully so that they could be used on future occasions by students who had similar difficulties.

The class was learning about map coordinates and she made a worksheet which took the work in small steps. It asked Linda and Julie first to find a particular number down the side of a very simple map on the worksheet, then the number across the top, and then to discover where they met and write down the name of the place in a space on the worksheet. This exercise was repeated for three different places marked on the map.

They were then asked to look at the map the rest of the class were studying and do the same thing. They managed the worksheet quite well without much help from Stephanie, who was able to concentrate on other members of the class. They were then able to transfer the skill successfully to the map that the others were using.

basic process in mathematics. For example, a student who continually writes the past tense by simply adding a 'd' to the word has not grasped the need to add 'ed'.

We have already looked at motivation for learning. It is particularly important to look at what motivates these students and to use this to help them to learn in appropriate areas. What is needed is work designed to help them to develop appropriate strategies for learning, so that they gradually become more capable learners. All students need this teaching but in some ways the need to provide this for slow learners is greater than it is for others, because of the limited amount of time you have to work with them.

Students with low ability tend to need short-term goals. You are more likely to be successful in teaching such a student if you identify clear objectives, which you share with the student and which can be achieved with one lesson, or within an even shorter period. You then give praise when the objectives are achieved and perhaps record achievement somewhere for the student to see.

If you teach in a school where classes are of mixed ability it is likely that there will always be students of low ability in your class. It is therefore worthwhile to make specific material for them. This material can be used many times.

Case study 9

Maggie had a year 7 class which included one boy, Robert, who, while appearing to be reasonably intelligent in the answers he gave in class, had considerable difficulty whenever he was asked to read or write. He was having help with this from the special needs department but, in the meantime, Maggie was concerned to see that he learned in her religious education class. She arranged for him to sit next to another boy who was a rather better reader, so that he could help Robert when they were asked to read in class. She also arranged for Robert to tape some of his written work and as often as possible she got this typed out and found odd minutes during the next class to get Robert to read it through. The work he produced in this way was of quite high quality and he was very pleased to see it in type.

As Robert became more confident, she suggested that he wrote out some of his work after taping it, doing the best he could with the spelling and punctuation. She then kept a record of the main mistakes he had made, looking for patterns so that she could help him to improve. Gradually he became able to write more and his reading improved with the help he was getting from the special needs department. By the end of the year he was able to do the written work of the class. He still made a number of mistakes but they were gradually becoming fewer.

If you add to this a little at a time and start with material you know you will need time after time, you gradually build a collection, and this makes it easy to provide for students at the right level. The same approach is needed for very able students. Ideally, this should be done at department level, so that all members of the department have access to such material as they need it.

Students with outstanding ability

The code of practice does not deal with students with exceptional ability, but you may have in your classes some students who are far more able than the average. These students have special needs of a different kind and may need individual programmes for some work. From time to time you may encounter a student who is so far ahead of the group that he or she needs an individual programme for almost everything, or at least a variation of the class or group programme.

Fontana (1994: 43) notes that such students can seem a threat to the teacher. They ask awkward questions, pick up mistakes by the teacher and may know more than the teacher about some aspects of the work. 'Only by recognising and welcoming these abilities, and by accepting that the attempts at self-assertion are natural and justified, will the teacher come to terms easily with the child.'

It is tempting to believe that such students are easy to identify and do not need any extra help because they can get on by themselves. The evidence from a number of studies suggests that this is not the case; some gifted students use their ability to hide their gifts and not all of them are known to their teachers, particularly if they are disinclined to conform and do as they are told. HMI stresses the importance of 'pupils being encouraged to think for themselves, to ask questions, to take some responsibility for their own learning and to contribute ideas' (DfE 1992: 16).

If you want to be sure that you are catering for students of outstanding ability you need to do the following:

- Develop your skill in identifying such students. Look particularly for the student who is unusual in some way, asks unusual questions or has original ways of looking at things. Where you have queries about such a student, ask if he or she can be seen by an educational psychologist.
- Make sure that your overall programme is rich and varied enough for latent gifts to emerge. Some people only reveal their gifts if the circumstances are right and when something strikes a chord for them.
- Consider possible teaching approaches for a student of outstanding ability. Try to ensure that you ask questions and present material at a variety of levels and that you include open-ended questions in any questioning session. Note the students who come up with unusual answers.
- Assess carefully levels of ability and stages of development within your classes. Examine the ways in which you check on the abilities and stages of

development of your students. Is it possible that you have students who could do much more demanding work than you are giving them? It may be a good idea to go through the registers asking this question, and then to check up on any students whom you think may have more ability than is apparent, by talking further with them and looking at their work.

- Organize work at different levels. With any work you plan to do with whole classes, see that there are, within the plan, opportunities for doing more or doing work which is more demanding. Very able students do not necessarily want the next stage of the work which is in hand, although it may sometimes be appropriate to go on to the next level in the National Curriculum. They are often able to do more than their peers and can enjoy a richer programme, involving their own investigations or ideas that you or they suggest. It is a waste of any student's time to do more of work that is already mastered, although it can sometimes be difficult to avoid this.
- Try building a collection of material for the faster workers that is challenging. Look for stimulating resource material which is relevant to the work in hand. It multiplies the material available if a group of teachers in a department collaborate in making and collecting such material and share it.
- Review worksheet and task card material from time to time to see if you can make it more demanding and stimulating for very able students.

We noted that students with learning problems need to be encouraged to become independent learners, as much as, if not more than, other students. Students of high ability have a particular need to acquire learning skills, so that they are able to work independently and are not too dependent on a busy teacher.

Case study 10

David demonstrated his ability in English from an early stage in the school. His written work was nearly always of outstanding quality, showing a maturity and command of language which was a long way beyond the usual standard for his age group. He also read widely and made very perceptive comments about the work being read in class.

His English teacher, Michael, soon recognised that here was a boy of exceptional ability and he took time to talk with David about his interests and particularly about the books he read. He made suggestions about other books that he thought David would enjoy and encouraged him to write for his own satisfaction and enjoyment, offering to discuss anything David wrote that he was prepared to show his teacher. He made a point of talking with David about his reading whenever he could, encouraging him and discussing what they both thought about the books.

Students whose home language is not English

Many schools now have students whose home language is not English. In many cases this is no problem because these students have spent all their school lives in British schools and have acquired English as it is spoken in their home area. However, you may have a few students for whom this is not the case, who find English difficult. The mistakes they make will reflect their home languages. By collecting errors over a period you can begin to see what needs teaching. For example, many Asian languages do not have an equivalent word to 'the', and students will tend to omit it in their writing. They may have problems with tenses and find some sounds difficult to pronounce and therefore to spell. When you prepare worksheets for such students and for students who have learning difficulties, it is wise to avoid not only difficult words which are not part of the technical vocabulary you want to teach but also such things as the passive voice and long sentences with many clauses.

SPECIAL NEEDS AND THE NATIONAL CURRICULUM

Work with students with special needs took on a new challenge with the advent of the National Curriculum. The National Curriculum Council's guidance paper, *A Curriculum for All*, starts with the statement 'All pupils share the right to a broad and balanced curriculum, including the National Curriculum.' This document makes it clear that it sees all pupils working towards appropriate points in the curriculum, even if some spend a very long time getting to each point. It also makes it clear that all pupils are intended to follow a curriculum that is wider than the National Curriculum.

Many teachers find it difficult to provide for students with learning difficulties because their training did little to prepare them for this kind of problem. There is nothing mysterious about the skills needed, however. They are an extension of the skills needed by every teacher and can be learned by anyone ready to make the necessary effort.

Successful work with students with learning problems

It may be helpful to look at the factors associated with successful work with students with learning problems. The school is most likely to be successful in teaching such students if appropriate teachers:

- study them as individuals with interests and a preferred style of working, and make a careful diagnosis of the nature of their problems;
- devise a programme for each student to meet the needs revealed by the diagnosis, and involve the student in setting and achieving realistic short-term goals;
- break down the necessary learning into steps which are small enough for the student to take successfully, but which also have purpose in his or her

eyes and involve decision-making and thinking and are not overdependent on memory;

- provide different forms of recording on occasion (for example, a student who has considerable difficulty in writing might be encouraged to record his or her work on tape);
- enable each student to see his or her own progress and reinforce learning, including the behaviour you want, by specific praise and encouragement and perhaps by charting progress in some way so that the student can see how he or she is doing;
- provide opportunities for each student to learn to take responsibility and become independent;
- provide genuine opportunities for these students to contribute to the life and work of their classes;
- keep careful records and review progress regularly, often involving the students themselves;
- maintain a positive attitude in all circumstances and provide many opportunities that are more likely to lead to success than failure;
- be patient and sympathetic and try to give the student the idea that you believe in his or her ability to succeed.

While a number of these points are more relevant for the special needs teacher than the subject teacher, they are pointers to the subject teacher as to how to deal with students with special needs. Initially this kind of differentiation is very difficult to achieve, but it becomes easier as material is built up and you become more skilled at recognizing the needs of individuals.

It is possible to take a positive approach even in the areas in which a student is weak. Most students are anxious to do well, and if you can get a student to join you in setting targets and achieving them in a given time, you enable that student to work positively to improve and add to achievement.

It would probably be fair to say that many people with disabilities can, if motivated, do more than other people think they can; this should be encouraged. Older students, in particular, need to be encouraged to be helpful and to treat students with disabilities as they would other students, except where their disability requires particular attention. In the main, the way students with special needs are treated by other students will come from the example set by the school staff. Look for opportunities for students with disabilities to contribute to the life and work of their classes.

The students we have been considering may or may not be a problem to the teacher. They may give you a permanently guilty conscience because you feel you should be doing more, but they will not necessarily disrupt the work of the class. Some of them and some other students will be disruptive, and you need to consider these students as individuals too.

Although there is provision in the Education Reform Act 1988 for disapplication of the National Curriculum for certain students under particular circumstances, it is clear from *A Curriculum for All* that this provision is not intended to be used to any great extent. The task of the teacher is therefore to seek ways of helping all students to achieve.

From your point of view, while it is valuable to know the causes of a particular difficulty, the more important question is how to deal with it. Partly, this means knowing enough about it to know what is possible and what is impossible. It is easy to be so concerned by what you discover about a student's background and so sympathetic towards him or her that you give too little attention to learning needs. The fact that Jim lives daily with violence and family rows might make you sympathetic when he finds it difficult to concentrate, but it may be that the most helpful thing you can do is to help him to succeed in learning. Every teacher needs to be a sympathetic human being, but no teacher has enough time to be a psychologist as well. It is generally better to concentrate on the professional task of being a teacher, showing human understanding as part of your everyday relationship with students.

Checklist 10 – Individual students

- Which students in my classes need to be treated individually for some of the time because of their special needs?
- How much do I know about the problems of each of them?
- Am I providing work for them which meets their needs?
- Am I creating situations where students with special needs experience success?
- Have I organized work so that students with special needs do not waste time?
- Have I any students of outstanding ability?
- Am I providing work which meets their needs and makes demands on them?

FURTHER READING

Ainscow, M. and Tweddle, D.A. (1988) *Encouraging Classroom Success*. London: Falmer. Gives descriptions of methods of dealing with children with special needs.

Denton, C. and Postlethwaite, K. (1985) *Able Children: Identifying Them in the Classroom*. Windsor: NFER-Nelson. An account of research with exceptionally able students in secondary schools.

Department for Education (1994) *Code of Practice on the Identification and Assessment of Special Educational Needs*. London: Central Office of Information. Gives details of what is now required from schools dealing with students with special needs.

Farnham-Diggory, S. (1992) *The Learning Disabled Child*. Cambridge, MA: Harvard University Press. Describes work with dyslexic students.

Greenhalgh, P. (1994) *Emotional Growth and Learning*. London: Routledge. A very clear account of problems of emotional growth and learning.

Marjoram, T. (1988) *Teaching Able Children*. London: Kogan Page. Ideas and suggestions about work with able students.

National Curriculum Council (1989) *A Curriculum for All*. London: NCC. Suggestions for managing the National Curriculum with students with special needs.

9

THE ROLE OF THE GROUP TUTOR

In most secondary schools, nearly all members of staff have charge of a tutorial group, although some schools try to place newly qualified teachers alongside an experienced teacher as a co-tutor for the first year. Sometimes tutorial groups are within one year group, sometimes they cover two years and sometimes all the years of the main secondary school. They may also differ according to whether the school is streamed or banded. In some schools a tutor takes a group of students either all the way through the school or through part of it. Other schools change tutors every year. This means that each year the tutors have to get to know a new group of students, who will try them out much as they will try out subject teachers.

There are advantages and disadvantages to all these forms of organization, but some aspects of the role of the tutor are similar whatever the grouping, and some will differ. The tutor with an intake year group will have a different role from the tutor dealing with year 11; the tutor with a mixed age group will have a different role again. There will be differences, particularly with the older students, between a tutor group which consists of high-ability students and one dealing with low-ability students. Where the tutor takes a group through the school or part way through it, he or she gets to know the students very well and they get to know their tutor, but this involves knowing the particular skills and knowledge required at each stage in the school. The role will also differ according to the responsibilities of the teacher with overall responsibility for pastoral care. In some schools the tutor plays a major part in such matters as communication with parents, writing of references and similar activities. In other schools these are responsibilities for the head of year or head of a section of the school.

THE TASKS OF THE GROUP TUTOR

It is important in being a tutor, just as it is in being a subject teacher, to have a clear idea of the aims and goals you have for the tutor group. These are bound up in the tasks which one is expected to undertake, which are now detailed.

Get to know and care for students

The tutorial system, however it is organized, is intended to ensure that all students are well known as individuals by someone who sees their work across the curriculum and is concerned with their personal and social development. The National Commission on Education (1993) commissioned a survey of students in the early years of secondary school, and found that 44 per cent of year 7 students and 45 per cent of year 9 students said that they never talked individually to their form teachers about their work. This is a depressing finding, which teachers need to do their utmost to disprove.

Hamblin (1978: xv) describes pastoral care as follows: 'Pastoral care is not something set apart from the daily work of the teacher. It is that element of the teaching process which centres around the personality of the pupil and the forces in his environment which either facilitate or impede the development of intellectual and social skills and foster or retard emotional stability.' He stresses that the pastoral system should be integrated with the curriculum and that it is concerned with a socializing function.

It is not easy for teachers in a secondary school to get to know well all the students they teach, particularly for those teachers who are the sole representatives of their subject. The tutor system is intended to make up for this by ensuring that someone has an overall view of the work, behaviour and development of each student. This is a very demanding role. Blackburn (1975: 24) suggests that 'By observing the neighbourhood, by listening to the pupils and their parents, learning from his colleagues, the new tutor will be able to work from generalisation towards an understanding of the particular values and attitudes that each member of his group has learnt from home and from the local community.'

The forming of a relationship with each individual student in a tutor group takes time. Some students will stand out because they are very able or very forthcoming, and some because they pose problems. Others will be more difficult to know because they are quiet and retiring. You will, at various times of the year, receive information about each student's progress in each subject of the curriculum. You need to find time during the year to have a discussion with each student about his or her progress in relation to the record of achievement and the subject reports. Much of the work of the tutor can contribute to the self-image of the student, and it is important that this contribution enables students to develop positive pictures of themselves and raises their levels of aspiration.

There is much to be said for keeping, in addition to the official records, a file with a page for each student, and noting down with the date any interesting information about each, including notes about discussions with the student and his or her parents. Initial information for the file will come from the school records and, in the intake year, from primary school records, but this can gradually be added to so that you have a developing picture of each student. This is particularly useful in discussion with the student about his or her record of achievement and in the writing of reports. It also makes students realize that you really do know something about them. It will be important to make them realize that you keep such a record so that you can get to know them well and not as a kind of 'big brother' exercise.

A number of students in today's schools will be experiencing problems such as family break-up, or will be members of single-parent families. A few parents may be too busy with their careers to give much attention to the children or may be violent and punishing. All these problems and many variations of them have effects on the child at school, and the tutor needs to be alert for signs that all is not well with a student. It may be that the most effective thing the school can do is to ensure that the student makes good progress academically and knows that someone in the school knows and cares about the problems he or she is facing at home. It is important that there are good opportunities for students to talk to teachers in confidence.

Davis (1985) notes from his research into the way young people in the secondary school thought about their lives that 'Nearly all pupils, even those who spoke freely to many adults and enjoyed friendly relationships with their teachers, kept locked within them information, aspirations, disappointments, fears, doubts and questions which could profitably have been discussed with one or more adults.'

It can be helpful to remember that people do not always go straight to a serious problem. They may start by talking about some comparatively trivial thing, and it is only if you have the time and patience to listen further that you discover that this is a cover for a much more serious problem. This is particularly likely with parents, who may be sounding you out to see how sympathetic you are before committing themselves to talking about what really bothers them.

The tutor also cares for the students as a group, and should aim to get them to care for each other. Dean *et al.* (1984) describe an experiment in which students were led, through careful questioning, to identify areas of their work and behaviour which they wanted to improve. These were then shared with partners, and students identified specific goals for themselves and reported back on their progress after a period, using friends to help with evaluation of how far they were achieving their goals.

There is a good deal of evidence (e.g. Rutter *et al.* 1979; Reynolds 1985) that students have better attitudes to school when they are given responsibility. There are opportunities to give responsibility both in the subject classroom and in the tutor room. It is tempting to give responsibility to those who have shown that they can take it rather than those who need practice in being responsible.

You should try to give every student the opportunity to take responsibility from time to time.

Complete required records of students

Pastoral tutors have the task of maintaining the register, although this is being taken over in some schools by computers. You are responsible for the final form of the reports to parents, making a general comment and signing them as tutor when others have completed sections on different areas of curriculum. Schools will have their own record systems in which you, as tutor, will play a part. Tutors have an important role in helping students with their records of achievement.

Make students feel part of the school

This will be particularly important for the intake year, where the tutor has the task of introducing students to the school and guiding them as they get to know it. But it is still important as students grow older to work at developing positive attitudes to school. Blackburn (1975: 13) points out that 'Each pupil will form an overall picture, based on those things that he cares to select, of what the school is about and where he fits into it. The tutor can reinforce attitudes that have been expressed, he can help pupils to clarify what they are feeling and take a leading part in creating some of the responses that the pupils will make.'

As tutor, you represent the school and can interpret what it is about to the students by such tasks as explaining rules, talking about the way we do things in this school, encouraging students to take part in school activities, talking about the school's successes and what it offers to its students, encouraging the wearing of school uniform and so on. Gray and Freeman (1987: 156) make the point that 'Many schools are obsessed with finding fault with student dress but few take pains to help students to a positive self-image in the way they dress.' You also need to listen to the way students feel about what is happening to them and feed back to more senior staff any views which seem important. Games like setting up a desert island and considering what laws should be made are useful for helping students to understand the need for a community to have rules.

Everyone needs some praise and encouragement, and providing this is part of the tutor's role. Try to look for something to praise on many occasions and see that every student gets some share of praise. Students who are less able or more difficult in their behaviour usually have a low level of self-esteem and a greater need for praise and encouragement than those who are more confident. We have already noted that it is important that praise is genuine.

The tutor is part of the school communication system, passing on information to students and feeding back information from them to senior staff. Many schools use a tutor group notice board in addition to giving information verbally. This enables students to remind themselves of information given out, and can give them a chance to add their own notices if they wish.

Help students to organize themselves and their work

Students in their first years of secondary schooling need particular help in getting themselves organized for a much more complex pattern of schooling than they have experienced in the primary school. Different books and equipment have to be available for different lessons in different places. Books have to be taken home for homework and homework has to be completed and given in at various times. As their tutor you can help by giving them timetable information and by showing them how to make a checklist of what they need each day. A check on homework diaries and discussion with other teachers may reveal students who are having difficulty with getting homework organized. At a later stage, students may need help with revision and with organizing themselves for examination work.

Monitor student progress across the curriculum

If as tutor you are to know how students are doing across the curriculum, it is necessary to develop strategies for checking on what is happening. At the beginning of the year there will be information from the previous year's records and reports to parents at the end of term or year also give information. It may be a good idea to take in some of the exercise books of a few students each week to see how they are doing, and to take the opportunity to discuss these with the students concerned. This not only gives you a chance to monitor work but also makes it clear to students that you are concerned about their progress across the curriculum.

Deal with problems

Accounts of many incidents of misbehaviour as well as other problems will find their way to the tutor, who will be expected to do something about them. Marland makes the following point about the role of the tutor:

> No remote figure has the power to influence pupils' interests, attendance, work and behaviour in a way that a really close tutor can. A pupil is less likely to stay away from school if he knows that his tutor can make a pretty shrewd guess if it is a genuine absence (note or no note); he is less likely to be anti-social around the school if he knows he will have to justify his behaviour to his tutor.
>
> (Marland 1974: 78)

Many of the problems you will have to deal with will be problems of behaviour, but there will also be students who have personal problems of various kinds and need support in coping with them. These may range from quarrels with friends to bereavement or parents leaving the family. The tutor needs to be observant for the student who is clearly unhappy or disturbed, and sympathetic and supportive to those who are dealing with problems.

Much that was said about behaviour in Chapter 6 will be relevant for the tutor dealing with problems of behaviour. As tutor you have to deal with some of the problems at second hand, but you have the advantage of knowing the extent to which a particular student poses problems with particular teachers or more widely. If the problem is with particular teachers it may be possible to discover something about the situations that lead to misbehaviour. In some cases it may be possible to discuss these with the teacher concerned. In other cases it will be more a case of helping the student to modify his or her behaviour, perhaps by developing awareness of the situations which lead to problems.

Where the problem is more widespread, with many teachers complaining, more senior staff may be involved and there should be some agreement about how the problem is to be tackled. There is very often a pay-off to students who misbehave, perhaps in terms of admiration from peers or generally a wish to get attention; consideration of this may give a pointer to a way to change the behaviour. Another cause of misbehaviour is a threat to self-esteem, and the task here is to build up the self-image to the point where threats to self-esteem can be tolerated.

Some form of counselling may be part of the solution. Form tutors may also find themselves in a counselling role with students who have problems of many kinds – difficulties at home, with friends or in getting on with other people, for example. If the relationship with the form tutor is a good one students may look to him or to her for help with their problems.

Collins (1986: 21) defines counselling as 'the process whereby a person helps another person to clarify his or her own concerns in such a way that he or she is able to solve problems, make decisions, and learn more about his or her own strengths and weaknesses.' It is important in counselling to try to see from the point of view of the person being counselled. Empathy with the other person is essential, as is warmth and creating a climate of acceptance of the student as he or she is at the present time. You need to listen actively, making inferences from what is said, observing body language and trying to assess the way the other person is feeling.

The Elton Report makes the following comment about the need for counselling skills:

> We are convinced that there are skills, which all teachers need, involved in listening to young people and encouraging them to talk about their hopes and concerns before coming to a judgement about their behaviour. We are convinced that these basic counselling skills are particularly valuable for creating a supportive school atmosphere.
>
> (DES 1989: 114)

Someone counselling a young person needs to create a situation in which he or she will talk freely and can be helped to explore problems and find solutions. It is important to plan, so that there is sufficient time and privacy to enable the problem to be talked through to a solution. This is not easy to provide in school, but it is very important. This kind of discussion needs to end with a plan for action, if possible formulated by the student. Students may be helped by discussion in a group of young people who look together at some of the problems of growing up. There may be opportunities for this in tutorial time.

Hamblin (1974: 9) suggests that the counsellor sets out to encourage:

- the *growth of self acceptance* in the pupil;
- the *development of controls from inside* the pupil, rather than continuing his reliance upon external checks and pressures;
- the *learning of relevant and competent coping strategies* and of problem-solving techniques which are realistic and viable for that pupil.

One problem about forming this kind of relationship with students is that someone in a counselling role may hear confidential information, which should properly be passed on (for example, information about drugs in the

Case study 11

Donna was in trouble with several members of staff because she did the minimum amount of work and did it badly, although most teachers believed she had it in her to do very well. Marion, her form tutor, decided to have a discussion with her, and managed to find a time when she could talk to Donna without interruption.

She asked Donna why she worked so little and found that it was mainly because she had so many responsibilities at home, where she was the eldest of six children with a mother who was frequently ill. Marion discussed this problem with her head of year, and they decided that Marion would arrange to see Donna's mother and explain the problem to her to see if a solution could be found. Donna's mother agreed that it was important, now that Donna was coming up to GCSE, that she did well and was able to get a good job and contribute to the family finances. She also agreed that she would try to see that Donna had at least two hours each night free to do her homework, away from the attentions of her brothers and sisters. Marion then agreed with Donna that she would really work hard and try to get good examination results.

This all worked up to a point. Donna still found herself staying up late at night to help her mother with the chores, but her attitude changed because she felt that her problems were understood and this meant that she worked harder in school.

school or the anxiety of a student who has become pregnant). There is, on the one hand, a need to keep confidentiality and trust and, on the other, to act responsibly. The task is to try to persuade the student concerned that information should be passed on to someone relevant, who may be able to do something to help the situation. If you are unsure what to do, the best thing will be to consult a more senior member of staff without naming the student.

See that school policies are put into practice

Tutors are also important in putting school policies into practice. The behaviour policy and the policy on bullying, for example, need to be dealt with at the tutor group level. Students need to understand that it is not wrong to report bullying and that they need to support fellow students who appear to be bullied. Bullies need counselling as well as victims, and some of the more successful ways of dealing with them have involved getting the people they have bullied to talk to them about how they felt. You need to try to create a situation where students find bullying unacceptable and are prepared to protect victims and isolate bullies. It can be valuable to discuss with students what they can do about bullying.

Role play, which encourages students to see things from other people's point of view, may be helpful in dealing with students who bully, pose behaviour problems or have difficulty in getting on with their peer group. Forms of behaviour modification can also be valuable, but this must be something agreed by all the teachers involved. Many schools make use of an 'on report' system, whereby the student who poses problems has to get each teacher to sign his or her report form at the end of each lesson, stating that the student has behaved reasonably during the lesson.

It can be valuable to persuade such a student to set himself or herself targets to achieve and involve a friend in helping to achieve these. It is important in this context for the tutor to check regularly how far targets are being achieved and to develop a system with the student of recording how well he or she is doing. Progress must be noticed and rewarded with praise and, perhaps, at some stage by a letter to parents or a visit to the headteacher to demonstrate how well the programme is going.

Help students to develop appropriate study skills

Whether or not there is a PSE (personal and social education) programme and whether or not subject teachers help students to develop study skills, the tutor should do everything possible to help students to become independent learners. Subject teachers may be expected to help their students in terms of the particular subject. As tutor you can give help across the curriculum, particularly in terms of attitudes towards study. Some students 'look everywhere for a cause of failure, except their own study habits' (Hamblin 1978: 73). Taking notes, essay planning and writing and revising for examinations are topics that the tutor can profitably pursue. Students may need help with organizing their learning material so that what they need can easily be retrieved. Some students find examinations very threatening; discussion about examination anxiety may help this. Students, particularly those in the intake year, may benefit from discussion about homework and how to set about it. Thought needs to be given to how they can evaluate their work and progress. Discussion with the tutor about the record of achievement will help this.

Students need help with problem-solving and decision-making. They need to see that the techniques they are learning in technology have wider uses and can be applied to everyday life problems. They need to learn to weigh up the pros and cons in making a decision. This kind of exercise can be discussed in small groups or pairs, taking situations from real life or from newspaper stories. It will be particularly relevant for those students who have reached the stage of thinking out what they want to do with their adult lives.

Support the personal and social education development of students

Schools vary in whether they offer personal and social education as a timetabled subject or whether this is a matter for a tutorial period with group tutors. They also vary in the extent to which there is a programme for teachers to follow or whether much of the initiative is left to the teachers concerned. Dean (1993: 135) lists the following topics as those which might be covered at some stage in the school:

- settling into the new school, finding your way about, learning what to do, making friends;
- study skills, planning your time and work, homework, revision and examinations;
- social skills, getting on with other people, both adults and peers, how to behave in particular situations, male–female relationships;
- communication skills;
- group norms and the way we are influenced;
- health education, misuse of drugs, smoking, alcohol, fitness, nutrition, personal hygiene;
- education for parenthood;
- sex education, including the roles of the sexes in society;
- racism and the need to avoid stereotyping;
- authority and responsibility, the law, crime prevention;
- economic and industrial understanding;
- money management;
- personal interests;
- career guidance.

This is intended as a list of topics for a full personal and social education programme, but where such a programme does not exist, you may wish to select suitable topics from this list for your tutor group. The students may also suggest matters they would like to discuss. The time taken by the National Curriculum has made it more difficult to fit in work on PSE, although it is one of the themes that schools are asked to develop.

Collins (1986: 59) defines social education as follows:

Social education is . . . any organization of learning experiences primarily concerned with skills, knowledge and experience which help people to relate to each other and deal with the demands made on them by social systems. It is assumed that this can only be achieved if the learning experiences also help people to discover who they are, what they are capable of doing, and how they can develop themselves and contribute to society.

He goes on to state: 'When designing programmes teachers need to bear in mind that social education is not just about skills and knowledge. It is also about experience, feelings, attitudes, beliefs, values and achievements. It encompasses the inner lives of people as they strive to come to terms with emotions, dreams and new ideas.' He stresses the importance of the teacher as a role model.

If students are to lead happy adult lives they need to become skilled at making relationships with other people. They need the social skills to move easily in a range of social groups. For some this may mean learning straightforward pieces of behaviour such as how to introduce someone, how to greet people, how to eat a meal in a restaurant or how to carry on a conversation with an adult. They need practice, at an appropriate stage, in being interviewed for jobs. Drama and role play have a valuable part. Good social behaviour also comes from good social interaction and from group activity. Opportunities for planning and carrying out activities together give important social education. There is also value in residential experience.

The tutor needs to see that this kind of learning takes place in schools where it is needed and that students learn to converse intelligently. Students need many opportunities for talking about getting on with other people, particularly of the opposite sex. They need to be able to see things from the point of view of other people, and you can do much to help them to do this. This is particularly true when you are dealing with cases of bullying. When you are dealing with misbehaviour more generally, there is often the opportunity to try to help the student concerned see how other people felt about his or her behaviour. Part of social learning is moral development, and some of the discussion about decision-making can be discussion of moral dilemmas. This is valuable for helping students to sort out their thinking and learn to appreciate that others have different views on moral questions. Students are in the process of building a value system, and discussion is helpful to this.

Blackburn notes:

The growing person discovers what he is like by comparing himself with other people, by observing people's reaction to him and his to them, and by listening to what others say about him. The picture he forms continually changes as each new experience leads to new discovery . . .

The tutor as he discusses with pupils, has the opportunity to contribute in a more conscious way to the pupil's understanding of himself by drawing attention to the things he observes and leading the discussion so that the pupil is able to express what he thinks and feels.

(Blackburn 1975: 85, 86)

Another way of tackling behaviour problems, which has been successful in some schools, is to provide a contract for the student, setting out the responsibilities of the student on the one hand and of the school on the other. There needs to be an element of reward in what the school offers, and some schools have involved parents in rewarding their children if they can reach the goals they have agreed. In some areas there has been industrial involvement, with a particular firm guaranteeing a job at the end of schooling if the student in question meets certain goals.

As tutor you are in a key position over truancy, since it is you who is responsible for registration and will therefore be aware of unexplained absences. Some truants may be school phobics who frequently complain of various minor ills and use the medical room a good deal. It is worth investigating the reaction to school of such students. Some students absent themselves on particular days or from particular lessons; a study of the register and a discussion with the student may clarify the reason for this. Try to make students who have been absent for whatever reason aware that they have been missed when they return and that this matters to you and to the group. Talk to individuals about the foolishness of truanting, and have some discussion with them each time they are absent. Truants need support when they return to school, with opportunities to catch up on the work missed and an attempt to discover the reasons for staying away. Hamblin (1978: 206) notes that 'many pupils who truant see school as not only uninteresting but uninterested in them.' Remember that there are sources of help inside and outside the school.

Deal with parents

The extent to which a tutor deals with parents will depend upon the practice in the school. It is usual for parents visiting during school hours to be seen by the head, deputy head, head of year or head of a section of the school, since tutors will usually be teaching. However, there will be opportunities at parents' evenings to meet parents both in the subject teacher role and in the tutor role. It may be the practice to send letters home when a student does especially good work or poses particular problems, and it may be the tutor's responsibility either to send the letters or to draw the attention of the head of year or the equivalent to the need for such a letter.

When you meet parents it is important to remember that they may have valuable information to give you about their children, as well as hearing from

Checklist 11 – The group tutor

- How much do I know about each individual in my group?
- What are my goals as a tutor?
- Do my records really add to my knowledge of my group?
- How many of the students in my group are really committed to the school?
- How much do I know about how the students in my group are doing across the curriculum?
- How successful am I at dealing with behaviour problems in my group?
- How successful am I as a counsellor?
- How successful am I in my contribution to personal and social education?
- Are my students developing good study skills?
- Are my students developing good social skills?
- Are my students developing well as people?
- Am I managing to deal successfully with bullying?
- How often do members of my group play truant?
- Do I encourage parents to tell me what they know about their children, as well as telling them what I know?
- How good am I at observing students?

you about how the children are doing in school. Try to be honest but positive about students who pose problems. Giving parents a negative view of their offspring is likely to antagonize them and make them unready to help the school to improve their children's work and behaviour. There is nearly always something positive you can say about a student, and this is the best thing to start with. You then need to ask for parental cooperation to help the student in question to reach his or her potential, looking for very specific things that parents could do. You also need to say what you and other members of staff are doing to help the student. The parents may have ideas about the best way to handle the problems their offspring poses. Deal with parents as partners in the process of trying to help their children develop as people.

If you are dealing with parents who are angry about something that has happened to their child, try to avoid showing anger or defensiveness in return. Listen carefully to what they have to say, trying to see things from their point of view, before explaining the school's point of view. Then see if you can agree on a plan of action.

THE SKILLS OF THE TUTOR

The skills needed by the form tutor are much like those needed by the classroom teacher. You need to be skilled at observing and interpreting students' behaviour, good at communication, able to lead discussion, sufficiently knowledgeable about the curriculum overall to be able to discuss problems, good at counselling and able to maintain good records and deal with many aspects of the PSE programme. You need to be particularly skilled at detecting those students who need individual help for some reason and providing it appropriately.

Blackburn (1975: 98) sums up the role of the tutor as follows:

> The tutor creates a secure framework in which tasks are set and standards declared, against which pupils are able to kick and find that it stands firm. At the same time there is sufficient warmth and freedom in the relationship for the pupils to feel that they are able to talk with the tutor, knowing that they will be heard with sympathy and understanding.

FURTHER READING

Blackburn, K. (1975) *The Tutor*. London: Heinemann. Although this book is now old, the advice and suggestions given in it are still highly relevant.

Collins, N. (1986) *New Teaching Skills*. Oxford: Oxford University Press. This book covers many of the skills a form tutor needs in dealing with individual students. It makes useful suggestions about counselling and negotiating with students.

Dean, J., Waddilove, J., Adams, D., Chanter, T. and Betteridge, D. (1984) *Where Am I Going?* London: Schools Council. A series of accounts of work with groups of secondary school students to help them to set their own goals and work towards them with help from their peers.

Hamblin, D. (1974) *The Teacher and Counselling*. Oxford: Blackwell. This is a book written some time ago for teachers specializing in counselling, but containing much valuable information that is more general and still highly relevant.

Hamblin, D. (1978) *The Teacher and Pastoral Care*. Oxford: Blackwell. Marland, M. (ed.) (1974) *Pastoral Care*. London: Heinemann. Both these books are old but have much to offer form tutors today.

10

EVALUATION AND ASSESSMENT

Evaluation and assessment in school are part of the everyday practice of weighing up situations in order to decide what to do next. When you make professional judgements you need to be more objective than in everyday life and to think very clearly. We evaluate in order to assess past action and learn from it, so that new action can benefit from our experience. Evaluation implies a setting against values. This suggests that assessment might be regarded as a stage in evaluation where information is collected in order to compare it with standards of some kind.

THE PURPOSES OF ASSESSMENT

There are four major purposes of assessment:

- to assist the progress and development of students and teachers;
- as a tool for management;
- as a means of accreditation;
- for accountability.

To assist the progress of students

Teachers assist the progress of students by assessing their work in various ways. Formative assessment takes place continually in the classroom as you respond to student answers to questions or to student questions, as you observe and comment on work in progress and help students to think through problems. Summative assessment takes place as you consider and mark finished work and make comments. Both formative and summative assessment help you to identify students who need more help and students who could work faster and at a more challenging level. They also give you an idea of how successful you have been in teaching particular material, and the readiness of students for the next stage in learning. Assessment gives students feedback on how they are doing. Comparisons of the work of an individual over time give a view of whether a particular student is making progress, and this may help with motivation if the student can see positive development. Comparisons across the group or across year groups enable the teacher to make judgements about the progress of particular groups.

A problem about assessment for some students is that they may not be able to see much progress, and this may lead to their becoming disheartened. This can be helped by assessing for effort as well as achievement, and by giving differentiated work, so that all students can achieve at their own level. However, this then means that the assessments have different meanings. This is not an easy problem, and teachers need to be sensitive to the problems of low achievers and to give them as much encouragement as possible.

Capel *et al.* (1995: 227) stress the need to consider the quality of students' learning and the development of understanding:

> If the outcomes of learning are judged solely by the amount of information retrieved from a pupil then the importance of the quality of thinking has been ignored. It is possible to differentiate quality of pupil response by the extent to which the information given has been transferred and transformed by the pupils, i.e. that they are able to demonstrate understanding.

They suggest asking the following questions:

- Do I wish to assess my pupils' knowledge or understanding? How do I distinguish these from recall? Or am I more interested in my pupils' level of skill development?
- Did I find out what my pupils can do (their positive achievement) or was the assessment experience essentially negative, with low levels of success demonstrated by pupils?
- Are my assessments capable of showing individual progress, based on measureable performance, or do my assessments simply rank pupils against each other? (Capel *et al.* 1995: 265)

To assist the development of teachers

The main formal way in which teachers' work is evaluated is through appraisal, which is intended as a developmental opportunity. Teachers' reflection on and evaluation of their work in the classroom and their discussion with colleagues plays a very important but more informal part in their overall development. Appraisal normally involves an element of self-evaluation, observation of your teaching by a colleague and an appraisal interview in which work and progress are discussed. The value of this must depend upon the skill with which the classroom observation and the interview are carried out, but many teachers have found appraisal helpful in developing their work and this is particularly the case for those in the early years of teaching. It is discussed in greater detail in the next chapter.

Inspection is also about development at a school level, which in turn means the development of teachers. Many inspectors will give teachers some individual feedback, which may be helpful, and there will also be a good deal of information to be extracted from the verbal and written reports.

Assessment as a tool for management

Assessment assists management at school, department and classroom level. At the school or department level, decisions have to be made about which teachers teach which groups of students. This involves making judgements about the skills of teachers and the nature and problems of particular groups of students. Similarly, at classroom level you make decisions about the needs of students for particular kinds of work. You also make decisions about grouping students, perhaps by ability, by the contribution individuals seem likely to make to a group or by some other criterion. In all these cases this involves making judgements about the students in question.

Assessment as accreditation

Accreditation takes place not only through examinations but also through the writing of references for students and records of achievement built up over a period. Schools provide accreditation for teachers in the form of reports on those seeking promotion.

Accountability

Schools spend public money and are accountable to the community through their governing bodies for providing the best education they can for their students with the money they are given. The advent of four yearly inspections and the demand to make public inspection reports, as well as examination and test results and other information, has led much further to meeting demands for accountability than has been the case in the past. The task for individual schools is to interpret the information they are legally obliged to provide to parents and the community.

WHAT NEEDS TO BE ASSESSED?

If a school is really to assess the personal, social and academic development of each student, this is a very considerable task. Even within one subject area it is far from simple. Dennis may be able to compute numbers fairly accurately but be unable to apply this knowledge intelligently to problem-solving. Leonie may answer well in class but put up a poor performance when it comes to essay writing. Michelle may do everything well with apparent ease and very little effort, whereas Craig tries really hard and is not very successful.

In most subject areas there are factual materials to be learned, concepts to be understood and skills to be acquired. Some students manage the factual learning but find the concepts and skills difficult, while others manage the concepts but find the factual learning more difficult. Subject departments need forms of record that take all of this and subject specific aspects into account. There is a need to differentiate between attainment and effort; to demonstrate that some students make a great deal of effort with comparatively little result, some work hard and get results and others succeed without really trying.

Students need to acquire reasoning ability, demonstrate creativity, acquire positive attitudes, develop socially and personally. Some of these abilities will show themselves in subject areas. Others may be part of the record of achievement which each student builds up as he or she moves through the school.

A particularly difficult area to assess is cooperative work, since it is not possible to sort out the contribution of the individual members of the group. However, there are valuable lessons to be learnt from what happens in groups. Kerry (1981) suggests taping discussions from time to time and assessing what has been learned in terms of the content of the discussion and also about working in this way. He suggests asking oneself whether members of the group have:

- put forward tentative or hypothetical ideas and asked for comment;
- supported assertions with evidence;
- contributed evidence in favour of someone else's assertion;
- pointed out flaws in the argument or questioned 'facts' put forward by others.

One might listen for the exercise of leadership skills, the extent to which the group concentrated on the topic in hand, whether there were many irrelevancies, members who talked too much or were silent and so on. These questions will not provide grades or other scores, but they will provide guides to the teacher about the way in which groups are working and the aspects of group work that need further training.

METHODS OF ASSESSMENT

Whatever the method of assessment chosen, teachers need to be clear about the criteria by which they are making judgements. These will vary from one piece of work to another, and there is much to be said for sharing the information about criteria with the students.

Assessing by observation

The most basic form of assessment is observation. As people, we are all the time assessing other people and situations and making judgements about them. In schools teachers do this both formally and informally. All teachers, and particularly teachers in the group tutor role, observe the students in their classes and make judgements about them, and it is important that they are aware of their own prejudices in making informal observations. It is very easy, without being aware that one is doing it, to assume that members of the same family have similar characteristics or to stereotype West Indians, Asians, boys, girls, those with special needs or exceptional ability or working-class students.

Observation is assisted by questioning and listening to students. Teachers need to try from time to time to assess how much understanding there is behind a piece of work. This may not be evident from the work itself and requires discussion with the student to find out his or her thinking. You can also learn how much students know and understand from presentations in the classroom, from listening to group and class discussion and from watching and listening to role play.

Observation plays a particular role in the assessment of language ability. In every subject teachers make judgements on the basis of students' responses to questions and the questions students ask and comments they make. In modern language teaching the teacher must continually assess the language skills that students are developing. In English the teacher needs to make judgements about students' skill in spoken and written language.

Observation is important for group tutors, who will make judgements about personal and social development on the basis of student behaviour, on what other teachers say about students and on what they have to say about their own progress in the context of interviews for records of achievement.

A specific form of observation is looking at the work students produce, whether this is written work, creative art, musical composition or performance, physical activity, drama or dance. Whereas the informal judgements made about most observations in the classroom do not lead to marking of any kind, much work that students undertake is marked or graded in some way. The purpose of this is developmental, and it is particularly important for teachers and students to be clear about the criteria on which marks or grades have been awarded if students are to learn from them. A school and certainly a department should have a policy about marking, making it clear whether work is to be given marks or grades and encouraging teachers to comment so that students can learn from their good points as well as their errors. HMI, writing in the *The New Teacher in School*, found that 'Some teachers did not appreciate the need for supportive, encouraging and constructive comment, or the diagnostic purpose and value of marking in helping pupils to improve their performance' (DES 1987: 16).

Clough *et al.* (1984: 66) studied the way teachers assessed work and found that they felt that different combinations of marks, grades and comments were needed for different work. They also found a great variety of views about ways of marking among teachers, including differences of views among teachers of the same subjects. English and physical education teachers preferred a comment alone, or a combination of grade and comment. Mathematics teachers commented: 'marking out of a predetermined number prepares students for the sort of assessment involved in public examinations in mathematics.'

Some teachers felt that 'children look for and compare marks. They rarely read comments.' Other teachers thought comments helpful in de-emphasizing competition between pupils and in encouraging good work. They thought that comments without grades encouraged low-ability pupils whereas they were discouraged by continually getting low grades. They thought it useful to record comments made on students' work with the date. This provided information for references and reports.

The overall finding of this study was that teachers have a wide variety of views on assessing students' work, depending on their particular philosophy of education. The researchers questioned whether students knew how marks were awarded and for what. The matching of methods to purposes appeared to be somewhat haphazard. Teachers need to ask, 'do the methods of assessment fulfil the specific intended purposes?' Teachers also need to ask themselves about the purpose of marking particular pieces of work. What should be done about errors? Is the work being assessed for ability to write good English as well as for content? Not all work needs to be assessed for both at the same time. It may be encouraging on some occasions for a student who makes a number of errors to have work praised for its content and not covered in corrections, providing that care is taken over errors on other occasions.

Kyriacou (1986: 34) suggests that students read certain things into the marking of their work in addition to the obvious points: 'Written work that is carefully marked and quickly returned is not only effective in increasing pupils' understanding, but also in communicating to pupils the teacher's concern with their work.'

Tests and examinations

Every teacher needs to check that learning has really taken place. Tests and examinations are necessary to ensure that progress is really being made. There are four basic areas in which questions can be asked:

- factual recall;
- understanding of the concepts behind a piece of work;
- ability to apply what has been learned to new situations;
- the extent to which appropriate skills have been acquired.

When you are devising tests and examination papers you need to be clear about your purposes. Do you want to test in all four of these areas or only in some of them? What information do you want to gain by testing, and how will you use it? How do you intend to mark the tests or examinations? Will the answers to all questions have the same value, or will some carry higher marks than others? If you want to undertake a practical test, how are you going to organize it and assess what is happening?

There are a number of ways in which questions can be framed. For more able students, open-ended questions provide an opportunity to show what they can do. You may need more structured questions for less able students, such as sentence completion tests, true/false items or multiple choice questions.

Essays are used quite frequently in secondary schools as a form of test. They are notoriously difficult to assess, and different markers can come up with very different results. However, marking is helped if you are really clear about the criteria by which you are assessing. You may be looking for specific points in the essay. You may also want to penalize for grammar and spelling mistakes.

Where examinations have been given across a year group it becomes possible to check how your groups have done compared with other groups. It is possible in your group tutor role to see how students have done across the curriculum, but for this to be fair marks should be scaled so that they are really comparable. Very few schools do this, but it should be remembered that a subject like mathematics tends to have a much greater spread of marks than a subject like English. Students who are good at mathematics are likely to get higher marks in an examination than those who are good at English.

You may want to use a standardized test for some purpose, i.e. a test which has been developed with very specific aims in mind and tried out with large numbers of students. This will give you information against national norms, which can be very valuable as a yardstick for student performance. When you are selecting a bought test you need to be very clear about what you want to get from the results. Standardized test results should always be seen as one of several pieces of information about student progress. Sumner (1987: 12) makes the following point: 'The rightful place of tests in a set of assessment tools has to be justified not on grounds of objectivity, but on account of aptness for purpose.' He also points out that tests should be regarded as an estimate of performance, which may vary with the day on which the test is taken.

Some of your students will also be taking the national Standard Assessment Tasks (SATs). If you teach English, mathematics or science, these will be of particular interest to you and, like public examinations, will give you the opportunity to discover not only how each group did in comparison with other groups in the same year, but also how the students in your school did in comparison with other schools in the area and more widely. The results will be of interest to form tutors.

Student self and peer assessment

Clough *et al.* (1984: 60) make the following statement about students' assessment of their own work: 'We encourage pupils to take responsibility for their own learning, but the right to assess that learning is rarely extended to them. Pupils' perception of their attainment must surely be potentially useful for the purposes of informing both learning and teaching.' They found it not uncommon for students to underestimate themselves.

Students need to learn to assess their own work, and there should be times when they are asked to make their own assessment of their work against criteria given by the teacher or developed in discussion with the class. It is helpful for students to work in pairs or trios to assess each other's work and discuss its good and bad points.

Students' assessment of teaching

Students are very well placed to assess the quality of the teaching they are receiving. This need not be carried out in a way that embarrasses the teacher. A questionnaire or a discussion asking questions such as 'did you understand this piece of work, what did you enjoy about it, what did you dislike about it, what did you find difficult, what did you find easy and what would you like to have more help with?' gives you useful information. A questionnaire has the advantage over discussion, in that you have replies from every student. You can use the answers as a basis for discussion.

RECORDS AND REPORTS

Every teacher needs to keep records of how each student is progressing. Kyriacou (1991: 121) suggests that this services the following functions:

- it should provide a useful basis from which reports to others (e.g. the pupils themselves, parents, other teachers) can be made;
- it should highlight any cause for concern if a pupil's performance shows a marked drop compared with previous progress;
- it should facilitate the planning of future work with each pupil by building on previous progress and, in particular, by ensuring that progress is adequate in its breadth and depth of coverage and that areas requiring remedial work receive attention.

The teacher's record will normally include a list of marks or grades for the work undertaken, with the dates when each piece of work was done. There should also be some comments about about what you have noticed about particular students' work as you marked it. One way of providing for this is to use a loose leaf file for recording marks, with pages cut back to reveal the class list as well as spaces for marks or grades for each set of work. The cut back pages enable you to keep any other pieces of information you wish, such as the form tutor of each member of the class, and to add comment against each student's name when you want to do so. It is important to date such entries so that you can see development over a period. You can also use this as a register for checking who is present at each meeting of the class in question.

Schools will have their own systems and policies for keeping records of students. Three are mandatory:

* a record passed from the primary to the secondary school stating the level the student has reached and giving SATs results;
* a record of achievement to be maintained by students and teachers throughout the time the student spends in school;
* reports to parents giving information about test and examination results of their own children, and comparative information about results of students of the same age.

In addition to these, the school will need to keep its own records of students and their progress. These are likely to include some background information where this is relevant, plus regularly updated information about progress in all aspects of the life and work of the school. These records will be kept by group tutors and will complement the records of achievement.

The fact that it is now compulsory for primary schools to send on a record for students transferring, which gives information about how far they have progressed, means that the secondary school can avoid covering the same ground again. Records coming into the secondary school from the primary school now contain information about how well individual students did in the SATs, as well as assessment by teachers. This has implications for how secondary school teachers work with the intake year. The SATs results may be used as a basis for banding and/or setting, or you may have students in your classes who are defined as being at different stages in the core subjects of English, mathematics and science. If you teach these subjects or subjects that make much use of written and spoken English, you may need to be prepared to differentiate work. Whatever your subject, it is important that you look at the records of students coming into your classes. It would be particularly wise to look at the records of any students who pose problems. Form tutors need to be very familiar with the records of the students in their groups.

Some teachers take the view that they do not want to be biased about new students by reading what someone else has said about them. This makes sense if what is said is merely opinion, but if, as is intended, the information is about work covered and progress in the National Curriculum, it is wasteful of everyone's time not to know what has been done and the stage students have reached.

It should be remembered that teachers' records are only partially confidential. Parents and older students can ask to see them, and they can be demanded by a court of law if necessary. It is therefore essential that you can substantiate anything you write down.

Records of achievement

Every school has to enable students and teachers together to compile an individual record of achievement for each student. In 1984 the Department of

Education and Science made a policy statement about this, planning that it should be made compulsory by 1990. This statement makes the following points about the purposes of records of achievement.

- Recognition of achievement. Records and recording systems should recognize, acknowledge and give credit for what pupils have achieved and experienced, not just in terms of results in public examinations but in other ways as well.
- Motivation and personal development. They should contribute to pupils' personal development and progress by improving their motivation, providing encouragement and increasing their awareness of strengths, weaknesses and opportunities.
- Curriculum and organization. The recording process should help schools to identify the all-round potential of their pupils and to consider how well their curriculum, teaching and organization enable pupils to develop the general, practical and social skills which are to be recorded.
- A document of record. Young people leaving school or college should take with them a short, summary document of the record, which is recognized and valued by employers and institutions of further and higher education (DES and Welsh Office 1984: 3).

Cawdron and French (1989: 3), in a handbook issued by Haringey local authority for its teachers, suggest that the summative record should:

- contain only positive statements;
- be based upon evidence compiled during the formative process and place achievements with a context;
- be issued at a time appropriate to the student;
- provide evidence to ensure progression into further education, employment or training;
- be presented in such a way as to be easily understood by users, including parents, employers and college admission tutors.

The record of achievement involves the form tutor in discussion with each individual student for a regular review of work and progress. It provides an opportunity for the student to record experience and achievement outside the school, such as work with youth groups, physical activity, special contributions in the home and so on. The tutor has an important responsibility to encourage the collection of evidence, review work and record achievement.

The major task for tutors in connection with the record of achievement is the interview. You need to prepare carefully for this, noting the points you particularly want to make. Avoid a seating situation where there is a barrier, such as a desk, between you and the student, and try to arrange things so that there will be no interruptions. Remind the student that the interview is confidential and start with a discussion of the present, leading into the past and the future. Try not to talk too much yourself, but get the student to talk about how he or she views progress and agree some goals for the future which you can review at the next interview. Make some notes after the interview, especially of the goals agreed.

Reports to parents

The school has a responsibility to give parents regular reports on how their children are doing in school relative to others of their age. Each school will have its own system for doing this. Writing reports for parents is not an easy task. It is sometimes a matter of trying to sound positive when you feel fairly negative about the progress a particular student has made. A good principle is to ensure that it is possible to back any statement you make with concrete evidence. It is also difficult to summarize performance in a subject when the student may excel in some aspects and make poor progress in others.

A more positive approach to reports to parents is to see that what you say gives parents ideas about how they can help and support their child in his or her school work. If you are being critical, try to include some advice on how the student might improve. It is important to remember that what may be everyday language to you as a teacher may be jargon to parents.

ASSESSMENT AS DIAGNOSIS

Assessment involves continuous diagnosis of the problems students are encountering. In the first instance you will be looking out for students who have not understood or remembered the work you have been doing. This may be revealed in the way they answer questions, in their written work or in the exercise of practical skills. If many students show the same problem then you need to go over the work with the class, but if it is a matter of a few individuals then you need to look for an occasion to have a word with those concerned.

CONCLUSION

Hull (1990: 100–1) makes the following general points about assessment.

- The assessment results should give you direct information about pupils' achievement in relation to objectives: they should be *criterion referenced*.
- The results should provide a basis for decisions about pupils' further learning needs: they should be *formative*.
- The scales or grades should be comparable across classes and the school if parents are to share a common language and common standards: they should be calibrated or *moderated*.
- The ways in which criteria and scales are set up should relate to expected routes of educational achievement, giving some continuity to pupils' assessment at different ages: the assessment should relate to progression.

Checklist 12 – Assessment and evaluation

- Am I clear about my purposes when I assess students' work?
- Do I make the criteria by which I am assessing a particular piece of work clear to students?
- What relevant information am I gaining by observing students in class?
- How quickly do I usually manage to return students' work after marking it?
- What am I gaining for the benefit of students from tests and examinations?
- Am I training students in self-assessment?
- Do I get feedback from students on their views of aspects of my teaching?
- Am I happy with the way I am recording student progress?
- Have I studied the relevant parts of the primary school records for the students I teach?
- Have I studied the records of students in my tutor group?
- Am I happy with the work I am doing with students on the records of achievement?
- Am I using assessment diagnostically?
- Am I developing my knowledge of what may reasonably be expected from students of different ages?

One of the difficult things for teachers at the start of their careers is that they have to learn what is reasonable achievement for students of different ages. This takes time. You can develop your skill in doing this by discussing your views of work with experienced teachers and by taking any opportunity you can to observe other teachers at work. It also takes time for an experienced teacher working with a new class to develop an idea of what is a reasonable expectation from different students.

Assessment and planning should be part of the same process. Your plans for the next piece of work should be affected by the results of your assessment of the previous piece of work.

SELF-ASSESSMENT AND THE TEACHER

Every chapter and some sections of chapters in this book have concluded with a checklist to help you determine your style and assess your own performance. The checklists are:

1 Lesson preparation.
2 Management planning.
3 The students.
4 The teacher's knowledge.
5 The teacher's skills.
6 Teaching strategies.
7 Classroom management.
8 Time management.
9 The use of space.
10 Individual students.
11 The group tutor.
12 Assessment and evaluation.

If you have already considered some of the questions in these checklists you will have done something to answer the question, 'How am I doing?' You may find it helpful to look back at the aims and objectives you had at the beginning of the school year and to consider how far you feel you have achieved them.

All that you do by way of assessment of students' work is valuable for you in assessing your own work. The need to reflect on teaching has been stressed at various points in this book and this is not only a matter of spending time thinking over what happened in various lessons, but also a matter of reviewing the assessments made of students' work from time to time to see what this information tells you about how well you have taught.

Your development as a teacher depends a good deal on your ability to be self-critical, to look at your own achievements and build on them. This is not just something for your early years in teaching, but a practice to continue year by year throughout your teaching career.

FURTHER READING

Clough, E.E., Davis, P. and Sumner, R. (1984) *Assessing Pupils: a Study of Policy and Practice.* Windsor: NFER-Nelson. An account of a study of assessment in schools.
Department of Education and Science and Welsh Office (1984) *Records of Achievement: a Statement of Policy.* Cardiff: DES/Welsh Office. The official statement about records of achievement.
Sumner, R. (1987) *The Role of Testing in Schools.* Windsor: NFER-Nelson. A description of all that is involved in the process of testing.

11

CONCLUSION

Teaching is an extremely complex job, and good teachers need to go on learning throughout their career, trying to manage things so that they avoid too much stress. This is particularly true at the present time, when changes are coming fast and there is much to learn and many pressures on teachers.

Sotto (1994: 167) notes how complex the task of the teacher actually is and he makes the following comment about it:

Anyone who has taught . . . knows that to teach well is very difficult, so it isn't possible to get it right each time. Always one is dealing with the most complicated things on earth – other people! So it isn't surprising if some lessons go wrong. In view of these circumstances, it seems best not to blame oneself too much when a lesson goes wrong, but to try to use the occasion to learn something from it.

Fontana (1994: 171) makes the following statement:

There is rarely a short-cut to the development of any worthwhile teaching skill and the skills of good class control and management are no exception. Much depends upon hard work, upon a belief in oneself, upon a willingness to learn from whatever experience happens to come along whether it be successful or unsuccessful, and upon a refusal to be discouraged.

INFORMAL LEARNING

Learning from normal teaching

In the early stages of teaching, every lesson is a learning opportunity, and the more you can find time to reflect and analyse what happened in a particular lesson, the more it will contribute to your learning. You may do some things as deliberate experiments, with the intention of learning something from them. You will learn from observing students, talking to them and finding out how they view what you have been doing with them. The learning possibilities are enhanced if a colleague can observe one of your lessons and give you some feedback on how you have been doing. This may be part of appraisal. You might like to tape parts of lessons and listen to the tape afterwards, asking yourself questions about the effectiveness of what you did and the evidence on the tape that you were effective.

It is perhaps worth remembering for yourself and for your students that failure is an important part of learning. Not all that you do will succeed, and it is important that you regard this not as something to be depressed about but as something to reflect on and analyse, so that you learn from what happened. Students are likely to be depressed if they do not achieve as well as they had hoped, and here again you need to explain to them that failure is a way of learning and that they should not be afraid to try because they might fail. This is particularly true for very able students, who may be unprepared to risk trying new things in case they fail.

Learning from discussion with colleagues

Your colleagues on the staff are one of your best sources of learning, and will generally be prepared to talk over problems with you and give advice. Don't be afraid to ask other teachers how they would have tackled a situation or how they would set about a particular piece of teaching or managing of students. Most schools allocate mentors to teachers in their first year of teaching. This provides you with an excellent opportunity to talk over the work you are doing with a more experienced colleague.

Learning from observation of another teacher at work

Take any opportunity you are offered to watch other teachers at work. Each will have his or her own style, which may be different from your style, but you can extend your ways of working by seeing how other people tackle things. Find out before the lesson what the teacher is planning to do and the ideas behind the work. It is a good idea to decide to look for particular aspects of the lesson since so much happens in any lesson, that it is difficult to keep track of all of it. Thus you might look particularly at how experienced teachers start and end lessons and deal with changes of activity. What do they do to avoid disruption and how do they deal with students who try to disrupt the lesson? What questioning techniques do they use and what variety of questions do they ask? How far did the lesson meet the goals the teacher had in mind and what did the teacher himself or herself think about what happened? You might look for the ways in which the teacher motivates the students, or at the quality of the interaction between teacher and students, at the way the teacher demonstrates his or her expectations of the class, or at the language used and its suitability for the students in question.

Similar learning opportunities are available when you work with another teacher. This has the added benefit of planning with someone else and learning how he or she approaches the task.

Taking part in working groups

Teachers learn from discussions with other teachers. One of the best opportunities for constructive discussion is to be part of a working group with a particular brief. It is likely to involve studying a particular problem the school wants to solve, coming up with suggestions for action. You will learn from the study of the problem and from the views of other teachers.

Learning from reading

Teachers tend to be too busy to read much, but both in your subject area and in the field of education generally development is taking place all the time, and you need to keep up with it as best you can. It pays to try to reserve a time for reading each week. Educational journals will often give you information about developments taking place and review books which describe them.

FORMAL LEARNING

Staff in-service days

Each school has a number of in-service days during the year, which offer an opportunity for the staff to work together, perhaps at forward planning or at a particular problem. Most schools and teachers find this a very valuable opportunity.

Attendance on courses

The opportunity to attend outside courses is limited by the money available to the school for this purpose, but you should have the opportunity to attend some course or courses each year. Most local authorities publish their lists of courses and make them widely available. There are also national courses, some run by subject or other associations and some by higher education and other institutions.

APPRAISAL

Purposes of appraisal

The Secretary of State for Education, in a 1990 letter to chief education officers, identified the following purposes for the appraisal of teachers:

- help teachers to identify ways of enhancing their professional skill;
- assist in planning the in-service training of teachers individually and collectively;
- help individual teachers, their headteachers, governing body and local education authorities (where appropriate) to see where a new or modified assignment would help the professional development of individual teachers and improve their career prospects;
- identify the potential of teachers for career development, with the aim of helping them, where possible, through appropriate in-service training;
- provide help to teachers having difficulty with their performance, through appropriate guidance, counselling and training; disciplinary and dismissal procedures shall remain quite separate but may need to draw on relevant information from appraisal records;
- inform those providing references for teachers;
- enhance the overall management of schools.

Dean (1991: 119–20) adds further points, including the following:

- it provides a means of coordinating the work of department and school;
- it provides an opportunity for praising what is good and dealing with unsatisfactory aspects;
- it provides the teacher with an opportunity to ensure that others know his or her work and for expressing views.

Self-assessment

Appraisal should involve some self-assessment, and most schools will have developed a pro-forma for this purpose. You may find some of the checklists in this book useful in this context. Many local authorities have provided suggestions to schools. Surrey, for example, suggests the following questions, among others.

1 Which aspects of your work have given you the greatest satisfaction over the past year?
2 What do you consider to be your strengths as a teacher, head of department, head of year etc.?

3 Which aspects of your work have not gone so well and would benefit from more work/training to improve them?

4 Identify any problems you have encountered which have prevented you from working as you would like. (Surrey County Council 1994: 35).

Classroom observation

Classroom observation by an appropriate colleague is an important part of appraisal, and should be valuable to you. There should be some agreement about the criteria that will be used for making judgements and an opportunity for discussion as soon after the observation as possible. There should also be some assessment of your performance as a tutor and a consideration of other contributions you have made to the life and work of the school.

The interview

The purpose of the interview is developmental. It should be positive and provide the opportunity for the interviewer to ask questions and give feedback. It should also give you a chance to give feedback to the management of the school on how you view it. There should be discussion of your in-service needs and possible provision for them, leading to some agreed goals for the coming period.

The report

The report on the interview should again be positive and developmental, and be agreed by the person being appraised. Most schools will have developed a standard form for this purpose, so that similar information is given to each person.

Your professional record

Schools vary in the records they keep of the work of teachers. You would be wise to keep your own record of your work, so that perhaps when, in a few years' time, you decide that you wish to try for promotion, you have a good record of the work you have done in your present school. You could include a record of the classes you have taught, work which has been particularly successful, your students' performance in examinations, extra-curricular activities in which you have been involved, in-service activities, both formal and informal, which you have experienced, your appraisal reports and any other information about your progress as a teacher that you think might be relevant at some time in the future.

INSPECTION

All schools are now to be inspected every four years. This means that you are likely to encounter an inspection before you have been teaching for very long. In some ways you will be better prepared for the process of inspection than your more experienced colleagues, since you will be used to having your lessons observed and commented on. Nevertheless, inspection is a stressful process for everyone, however good the school and the teachers.

The school will have a copy of the inspection handbook (1993, revised 1995) and from this you will be able to see what the inspectors are looking for. Many schools commission pre-inspection visits from their local advisory service so that teachers can be aware of anything they should be doing which is currently missing from their practice. It will be important to have all your paperwork up to date and your plans clearly set out. All the points that have been made earlier in this book about looking confident and acting confidently apply in this situation. You will, of course, want to show your work to the best advantage, but you would be wise not to attempt anything too different from your normal practice.

WORKING WITH COLLEAGUES

As a member of a teaching staff you are part of a series of teams, at a school level, within your department and as a form tutor. Much of the research on effective schools suggests that these are schools where everyone works together to support student learning. Even if you find that in your school there is not very much team work, you still have a responsibility to contribute as a team member and to support your colleagues.

Cohen and Manion (1989: 12) point out that in any organization there is an informal structure of relationships of which you need to be aware.

As well as the formal structuring of relationships among members of the school there is generally an *informal* organizational structure, that is a system of social relationships developed by members of staff outside any formalized requirements for their professional behaviour. It is through the informal organizational structure that communications about important decisions often become known to members of staff long before official pronouncements by the head.

In a similar way, you need to become aware of any particular quirks on the part of colleagues, such as having a favourite chair in the staff room or a special mug for coffee.

Your colleagues should be a source of valuable information for you on many aspects of your work. They will know the students well, and may have useful advice on how to manage more difficult characters. They will have tried many ways of teaching, and you can learn from observing them at work. You may meet cynicism and a depressed view of the life of a teacher, as well as enthusiasm and love of the work. If you are fortunate you will make friends who will influence your work as a teacher and enrich your social and professional life.

One way of encouraging other people to be helpful to you is to take any opportunity to be helpful to them. In any organization there are ways in which one person can be helpful to another, and it is always valuable to be a good listener. If you are not the only newly qualified teacher, you may find occasions when other new teachers want the opportunity to talk to someone who has similar experience. By listening to their problems you may find you are in the process of solving problems of your own. We all need to be appreciated, and new teachers may be able to offer each other some appreciation.

STRESS

Teaching is a stressful occupation. The many demands on a teacher throughout the school day are stressful in themselves. When these are added to the changes coming into education and the demands these make on teachers, it is not surprising that many teachers show symptoms of stress. There is also the problem that teachers are expected to be friends and helpers to students at the same time as being examiners and assessors. There is an element of conflict between these two roles which can be stressful. Teachers may also find themselves at variance with the values of their particular school. Society's attitude to teachers at the present time does not make life any easier. As Esteve (1989: 12) comments, 'If everything goes well, parents think that their children are good pupils, but if things go badly, they think the teacher is a bad teacher.'

Gray and Freeman (1987: 4) make the point that stress is in itself neither good nor bad. 'Stress can be stimulating or energizing, in which case it is positive and beneficial or it can cause feelings of anxiety, distress or discomfort; here it is a negative and harmful condition.' They go on to note the physical signs of anxiety that accompany stress. These include 'rapid and shallow breathing, increased heart rate, sweating, dryness of the mouth, nausea, insomnia, trembling, restlessness, feelings of weakness and inability to concentrate' (p. 6). Stress also shows in various emotions, such as anger, tension, depression and irritability, and in difficulty in making decisions.

Stress is said to be caused when there is an imbalance between the demands made on a person and his or her capacity for fulfilling them. However, some teachers perceive some circumstances as more threatening than others and make demands on themselves which they have difficulty in fulfilling. People who are highly ambitious, perfectionist and over-conscientious, who tend to be workaholics, are more likely to suffer from stress than those who are more laid back, relaxed and easy going.

Stress can lead to burnout. Kyriacou (1989: 27) notes that 'Teacher burnout refers to a state of mental, emotional and attitudinal exhaustion in teachers which results from a prolonged experience of stress. Such teachers are still able to function as teachers, but they have largely lost their commitment and enthusiasm for their work and this inevitably shows in aspects of their job performance.' Mancini *et al.* (1984) found that burned out teachers gave significantly less information and less praise to students. They also showed less acceptance of students' ideas and interacted with them less frequently.

Fontana (1994: 165) discusses the fear and anxiety that often causes stress in newly qualified teachers. He suggests that this is a normal response and that it helps to analyse the causes of the anxiety. He says: 'If we analyse the fear a little deeper, we may find that what actually prompts the anxiety is not so much the direct confrontation posed by the children as the teacher's fear of personal humiliation and being made to deal with it. That is the teacher's fear that there will be loss of self-esteem and loss of esteem in the eyes of children.' He goes on to suggest that one should deliberately slow down (fear makes us hurry), breathe more deeply before going to the lesson, concentrate on breathing and try to relax deliberately.

Woods (1989) suggests that among the people most at risk are inexperienced teachers who have not yet learned to cope with the dilemmas and contradictions of the teacher's role. Gray and Freeman (1987: 43) note that beginning teachers 'fear loss of face, loss of confidence, professional inadequacy, running out of work for the class to do, being unable to prepare adequately and so on . . . They also fear the reaction of older colleagues – and perhaps their peers – who may find that they are not doing too well in the classroom.'

It is evident from these studies that you need to take care to avoid stress. Kyriacou (1991: 137–8) suggests that you should first try to identify the cause of stress and see if you can do anything to lessen it. He states that 'the experience of stress is triggered by the perception of threat to your self-esteem.' You may be able to identify the particular situations which are threatening you, and in some cases it may be possible to do something about them. He suggests: 'Particularly useful are mental techniques, such as getting things in perspective, trying to see the humour in a situation, trying to detach yourself from personal and emotional involvement in a situation, and sharing your worries and concerns with others.' It is also worth remembering that you are more likely to feel under stress if you are tired, have a low energy level, are in poor health or feel dissatisfied with your job.

Other writers concentrate on activities outside the school which may relieve stress. Handy (1976) speaks of creating 'stability zones', which he describes as places for rebuilding energy reserves. Holidays and weekends, home and family, are important stability zones. It is valuable to be able to turn to some quite different activity or occupation. There seems to be some evidence that physical activity helps to minimize stress, whether it is a strenuous game or a mild activity such as gardening. Making things offers a way of relaxing. Relaxation techniques and meditation are also useful as ways of managing stress.

It is helpful to be able to talk through one's problems with a colleague, friend or partner. Handy suggests that routines are a way of coping with stress as well as a good way of managing time. They are particularly useful when you are tired and flagging and the habit can take over.

Capel *et al.* (1995) suggest that you should prepare for stressful situations when you are not under stress, visualizing what might happen and thinking about how you would deal with them. They also suggest identifying where you can get help and developing support systems of people with whom you can talk through problems.

However keen you are on your work, there is a case for finding time to do something different. You will be a better teacher if you find time to refresh yourself and perhaps meet people with other interests.

GOOD SECONDARY SCHOOL TEACHERS

Good secondary school teachers are enthusiasts in their chosen fields and keen to communicate this enthusiasm to students. They use a wide variety of teaching methods and are constantly seeking new ways to make learning an enjoyable activity and an effective one. They have developed a teaching style which encourages students to work hard for them, and in consequence their students achieve well and in many cases acquire an enthusiasm for the subject in question.

Good secondary school teachers like young people. They enjoy working with them and have an understanding of their culture. They respect them as people, are interested in their ideas and encourage their interests. They believe that students can do better than they themselves believe, and they somehow manage to convey that belief to students. They are nevertheless firm in the demands they make on students and skilled in identifying possible sources of problems before they occur. This is generally appreciated, there are in consequence few problems of misbehaviour in class and a great deal of learning time is spent on task.

Students in the classes of such teachers have had good training in independent learning. They are able to organize themselves and their work. They have good study skills, read intelligently, ask good questions and present work well.

Good teachers are well organized people who use time profitably. They have systems for dealing with many aspects of their work, which make things run smoothly. They prepare lessons carefully and are skilled in dealing with changes of activity.

Teachers who have rooms of their own, in which most of their teaching takes place, keep them well organized. Such rooms are attractive, rich in resources and good advertisements for their subjects. There is often good display, both of students' work and of items of interest. Materials and equipment are carefully arranged so that students have easy access to what they need and can return what they have used to its right place without difficulty.

Good teachers are good learners. They are aware of the need to go on learning. They read widely and take every opportunity to go to appropriate courses. They experiment in the classroom and discuss their teaching with colleagues.

They are successful group tutors, taking personal interest in their students and caring for them. They provide good models for students, who respect them, enjoy their teaching and try to care for each other as the teacher cares for them.

They are involved not only in their own departments but in the wider setting of the school, contributing in many ways to its development. They see themselves as professional educators who work to keep up with what is happening in education and to see whether research findings have any relevance for the students they teach.

This picture is a demanding one. It is greatly to the credit of teachers in secondary schools that so many achieve something near it.

FURTHER READING

Cole, M. and Walker, S. (eds) (1989) *Teaching and Stress*. Milton Keynes: Open University Press. Analyses the causes of stress for teachers and suggests ways of tackling it.

Dunham, J. (1992) *Stress in Teaching*, 2nd edn. London: Routledge. Looks at causes of stress and at the symptoms caused by stress. Goes on to look at ways of dealing with it.

Gray, H. and Freeman, A. (1987) *Teaching without Stress*. London: Paul Chapman Publishing. Takes the view that there is stress in all organizations and looks at ways of avoiding it.

APPENDIX: Competencies expected of newly qualified secondary school teachers

This material is taken from Department for Education Circular 9/92 (1992). Crown copyright is reproduced with the permission of the Controller of HMSO.

Subject knowledge
2.2 Newly qualified teachers should be able to demonstrate:
  2.2.1 an understanding of the knowledge, concepts and skills of their specialist subjects and of the place of these subjects in the secondary curriculum;
  2.2.2 knowledge and understanding of the National Curriculum and attainment targets (NCATs) and the programmes of study (PoS) in the subjects they are preparing to teach, together with an understanding of the framework of the statutory requirements;
  2.2.3 a breadth and depth of subject knowledge extending beyond PoS and examination syllabuses in school.

Subject application
2.3 Newly qualified teachers should be able to:
  2.3.1 produce coherent lesson plans which take account of NCATs, PoSs and of the school's curriculum policies;
  2.3.2 ensure continuity and progression within and between classes and in subjects;
  2.3.3 set appropriately demanding expectations for pupils;

2.3.4 employ a range of teaching strategies appropriate to the age, ability and attainment levels of pupils;

2.3.5 present subject content in clear language and in a stimulating manner;

2.3.6 contribute to the development of pupils' language and communication skills;

2.3.7 demonstrate ability to select and use appropriate resources, including information technology.

Class management
2.4 Newly qualified teachers should be able to:

2.4.1 decide when teaching the whole class, groups, pairs, or individuals is appropriate for particular learning purposes;

2.4.2 create and maintain a purposeful and orderly environment for the pupils;

2.4.3 devise and use appropriate rewards and sanctions to maintain an effective learning environment;

2.4.4 maintain pupils' interest and motivation.

Assessment and recording of pupils' progress
2.5 Newly qualified teachers should be able to:

2.5.1 identify the current level of attainment of individual pupils using NCATs, statements of attainment and the end of key stage statements where applicable;

2.5.2 judge how well each pupil performs against a standard expected of a pupil of that age;

2.5.3 assess and record systematically the progress of individual pupils;

2.5.4 use such assessment in their teaching;

2.5.5 demonstrate that they understand the importance of reporting to pupils on their progress and of marking their work regularly against agreed criteria.

Further professional development
2.6 Newly qualified teachers should have acquired in initial training the necessary foundation to develop:

2.6.1 an understanding of the school as an institution and its place within the community;

2.6.2 a working knowledge of their pastoral, contractual, legal and administrative responsibilities as teachers;

2.6.3 an ability to develop effective working relationships with professional colleagues and parents, and to develop their communication skills;

2.6.4 an awareness of individual differences, including social, psychological, developmental and cultural dimensions;

2.6.5 the ability to recognize diversity of talent including that of gifted pupils;

2.6.6 the ability to identify special educational needs or learning difficulties;

2.6.7 a self-critical approach to diagnosing and evaluating pupils' learning, including a recognition of the effects on that learning of teachers' expectations;

2.6.8 a readiness to promote the moral and spiritual well-being of pupils.

REFERENCES

Adair, J. (1987) *How to Manage Your Time*. Guildford: Talbot Adair/McGraw-Hill.

Ainscow, M. and Tweddle, D.A. (1988) *Encouraging Classroom Success*. London: Falmer.

Barnes, D. and Todd, F. (1977) *Communication and Learning in Small Groups*. London: Routledge and Kegan Paul.

Bennett, N. (1992) *Managing Learning in the Primary School Classroom*. Stoke-on-Trent: Association for the Study of Primary Education/Trentham Books.

Bennett, N. and Carré, C. (1993) *Learning to Teach*. London: Routledge.

Bishop, A.J. and Whitfield, R.C. (1972) *Situations in Teaching*. London: McGraw-Hill.

Blackburn, K. (1975) *The Tutor*. London: Heinemann.

Brennan, W.K. (1979) *Curriculum Needs of Slow Learners*. Schools Council Working Paper number 63. London: Evans/Methuen Educational.

Brown, G. (1975) *Microteaching*. London: Methuen.

Brown, G. and Armstrong, S. (1984) Explaining and explanations, in E.C. Wragg (ed.) *Classroom Teaching Skills*. London: Routledge.

Brown, G. and Wragg, E.C. (1993) *Questioning*. London: Routledge.

Bruner, J.S. (1966) *The Process of Education*. New York: Vintage.

Bruner, J.S. (1968) *Towards a Theory of Instruction*. Cambridge, MA: Harvard University Press.

Canter, L. (1979) Competency based approach to discipline – it's assertive, *Thrust for Educational Leadership*, January, 11–13.

Capel, S., Leask, M. and Turner, T. (1995) *Learning in the Secondary School : a Companion to School Experience*. London: Routledge.

Cawdron, M. and French, J. (1989) *Equal Opportunities and Recording Achievement: A Handbook for Tutors*. London: Borough of Haringey.

Charlton, T. and David, K. (1993) *Managing Misbehaviour in Schools*, 2nd edn. London: Routledge.

Clough, E.E., Davis, P. and Sumner, R. (1984) *Assessing Pupils: a Study of Policy and Practice.* Windsor: NFER-Nelson.

Clwyd County Council (1983) *Equal Opportunities and the Secondary School Curriculum.* Mold, Wales: Clwyd CC.

Cohen, L. and Manion, L. (1983) *A Guide to Teaching Practice.* London: Methuen.

Cohen, L. and Manion, L. (1989) *A Guide to Teaching Practice,* 3rd edn. London: Methuen.

Cole, M. and Walker, S. (eds) (1989) *Teaching and Stress.* Milton Keynes: Open University Press.

Collins, N. (1986) *New Teaching Skills.* Oxford: Oxford University Press.

Crane, W.D. and Mellon, D.M. (1978) Causal influences of teachers' expectations on children's academic performance: a cross lagged panel analysis. *Journal of Education Psychology,* 70(1), 39–49.

Davies, W.J.K. (1978) *Implementing Individualized Learning.* London: Council for Educational Technology.

Davis, L. (1985) *Caring for Secondary School Pupils.* London: Heinemann.

Dean, J. (1991) *Professional Development in School.* Milton Keynes: Open University Press.

Dean, J. (1993) *Managing the Secondary School,* 2nd edn. London: Routledge.

Dean, J., Waddilove, J., Adams, D., Chanter, T. and Betteridge, D. (1984) *Where Am I Going?* London: Schools Council.

Denham, C. and Leiberman, A. (1980) *Time to Learn.* Washington, DC: National Institute of Education.

Denscombe, M. (1985) *Classroom Control: a Sociological Perspective.* London: George Allen and Unwin.

Denton, C. and Postlethwaite, K. (1985) *Able Children: Identifying them in the Classroom.* Windsor: NFER-Nelson.

Department of Education and Science (1981) *Education Act.* London: HMSO.

Department of Education and Science and Welsh Office (1984) *Records of Achievement: a Statement of Policy.* Cardiff: DES/Welsh Office.

Department of Education and Science (1985) *Good Teachers.* London: HMSO.

Department of Education and Science (1987) *The New Teacher in School: a Survey by HM Inspectors in England and Wales.* London: HMSO.

Department of Education and Science (1988) *The Education Reform Act.* London: HMSO.

Department of Education and Science and Welsh Office (1989) *Discipline in Schools: Report of the Committee of Enquiry Chaired by Lord Elton.* London: HMSO.

Department for Education (1992) *Initial Teacher Training (Secondary Phase).* Circular No. 9/92. London: DfE.

Department for Education (1994) *Code of Practice on the Identification and Assessment of Special Educational Needs.* London: Central Office of Information.

Dillon, J.T. (1994) *Using Discussion in the Classroom.* Buckingham: Open University Press.

Dunham, J. (1992) *Stress in Teaching,* 2nd edn. London: Routledge.

Dunne, E. and Bennett, N. (1990) *Talking and Learning in Groups.* London: Macmillan.

Earley, P. and Kinder, K. (1995) *Initiation Rights: Effective Induction Practices for New Teachers.* Slough: National Foundation for Educational Research.

Edwards, D. and Mercer, N. (1987) *Common Knowledge.* London: Methuen.

Esteve, J. (1989) Teacher burnout and teacher stress, in M. Cole and S. Walker (eds) *Teaching and Stress.* Milton Keynes: Open University Press.

Farnham-Diggory, S. (1992) *The Learning Disabled Child.* Cambridge, MA: Harvard University Press.

Fontana, D. (1985) *Classroom Control*. London: British Psychological Society and Methuen.

Fontana, D. (1993) *Managing Time*. Leicester: British Psychological Society.

Fontana, D. (1994) *Managing Classroom Behaviour*. Leicester: British Psychological Society.

Galton, M. (1989) *Teaching in the Primary School*. London: David Fulton.

Galton, M. and Delafield, A. (1981) Expectancy effects in primary classrooms, in B. Simon and J. Willcocks (eds) *Research and Practice on the Primary Classroom*. London: Routledge and Kegan Paul.

Glasser, W. (1969) *Schools without Failure*. New York: Harper and Row.

Gnagey, W. (1975) *Maintaining Discipline in Classroom Instruction*. London: Collier Macmillan.

Goodlad, S. and Hirst, B. (1990) *Explorations in Peer Tutoring*. Oxford: Blackwell.

Graham, J. (1994) *Gender Differences and GCSE Results*. Stafford: Centre for Successsful Schools, Keele University.

Gray, H. and Freeman, A. (1987) *Teaching without Stress*. London: Paul Chapman Ltd.

Gray, J. and Richer, J. (1988) *Classroom Responses to Disruptive Behaviour*. London: Macmillan Education.

Greenhalgh, P. (1994) *Emotional Growth and Learning*. London: Routledge.

Hamblin, D. (1974) *The Teacher and Counselling*. Oxford: Blackwell.

Hamblin, D. (1978) *The Teacher and Pastoral Care*. Oxford: Blackwell.

Handy, C. (1976) *Understanding Organisations*. Harmondsworth: Penguin.

Hargreaves, D.H. (1982) *The Challenge for the Comprehensive School: Culture, Curriculum and Community*. London: Routledge.

Hargreaves, D.H. (1984) *Improving Secondary Schools: Report of the Committee on the Curriculum and Organisation of Secondary Schools*. London: Inner London Education Authority.

Hull, J. (1990) *Classroom Skills – a Teachers' Guide*. London: David Fulton.

Ingleson, S. (1982) Creating conditions for success in mixed ability classes, in M. Sands and T. Kerry (eds) *Mixed Ability Teaching*. London: Croom Helm.

Jackson, K.E. (1975) *The Art of Solving Problems*. London: Heinemann.

Kelly, A.V. (1974) *Teaching Mixed Ability Classes: an Individualised Approach*. London: Harper and Row.

Kelly, A.V. (1989) *Gender Differences in Teacher–Pupil Interaction: a Meta-analytic Review*. Research Papers in Education. London: Routledge.

Kerry, T. (1980) *Effective Questioning*. Nottingham: Nottingham University School of Education.

Kerry, T. (1981) Talking, the teacher's role, in C. Sutton (ed.) *Communication in the Classroom*. London: Hodder and Stoughton.

Kerry, T. (1982) The demands made on pupils' thinking in mixed ability classes, in M. Sands and T. Kerry (eds) *Mixed Ability Teaching*. London: Croom Helm.

Kounin, J. (1970) *Discipline and Group Management in Classrooms*. New York: Holt, Rinehart and Winston.

Kyriacou, C. (1986) *Effective Teaching in Schools*. Oxford: Blackwell.

Kyriacou, C. (1989) The nature and prevalence of teacher stress, in M. Cole and S. Walker (eds) *Teaching and Stress*. Milton Keynes: Open University Press.

Kyriacou, C. (1991) *Essential Teaching Skills*. Oxford: Blackwell.

Lambley, H. (1993) Learning and behaviour problems, in T. Charlton and K. David (eds) *Managing Misbehaviour in Schools*, 2nd edn. London: Routledge.

Lawrence, J., Steed, D. and Young, P. (1984) *Disruptive Children, Disruptive Schools.* London: Routledge.

Lewin, K. (1947) Frontiers in group dynamics, 1. Concept, method and reality in social sciences: social equilibria and social change, *Human Relations*, 1(1), 5–41.

Mancini, V., Wuest, D., Vantine, K. and Clark, E. (1984) The use of instruction and supervision in interaction analysis on burned out teachers: its effects on teaching behaviours, level of burnout and academic learning time, *Journal of Teaching in Physical Education*, 3(2), 29–46.

Marjoram, T. (1988) *Teaching Able Children.* London: Kogan Page.

Marland, M. (ed.) (1974) *Pastoral Care.* London: Heinemann.

Marland, M. (1975) *The Craft of the Classroom: a Survival Guide.* London: Heinemann.

Martinson, J. (1994) Keen at seven, lost by eleven, *Times Educational Supplement*, 18 March, 14.

Moon, J. (1985) *A Time: the Busy Manager's Action Plan for Effective Self-management.* New York: Van Nostrand Reinhold.

Morgan, N. and Saxton, J. (1991) *Teaching Questioning and Learning.* London: Routledge.

Mortimore, P., Simmons, P., Stoll, L., Lewis, D. and Ecob, R. (1988) *School Matters.* London: Open Books.

Mussen, P.H., Conger, J.J. and Kagan, J. (1963) *Child Development and Personality.* London: Harper and Row.

National Commission on Education (1993) *Learning to Succeed: a Radical Look at Education Today.* London: Heinemann for the Paul Hamlyn Foundation.

National Curriculum Council (1989) *A Curriculum for All.* London: NCC.

Neill, S. and Caswell, C. (1993) *Body Language for Competent Teachers.* London: Routledge.

Newman, J. (ed.) (1990) *Finding Our Own Way: Teachers Exploring Their Assumptions.* Portsmouth, NH: Heinemann.

Ofsted (1993) *Handbook for the Inspection of Schools.* London: HMSO.

Parsons, J.E., Ruble, D.N., Hodges, K.L. and Small, A.V. (1976) Cognitive-developmental factors in emerging sex differences in achievement related expectancies, *Journal of Social Issues*, 32(3), 47–61.

Piaget, J. and Inhelder, B. (1969) *The Psychology of the Child.* London: Routledge and Kegan Paul.

Purkey, W. (1978) *Inviting School Success: a Self-concept Approach to Teaching and Learning.* USA: Wadsworth.

Reid, K., Hopkins, D. and Holly, P. (1987) *Towards the Effective School.* Oxford: Blackwell.

Reynolds, D. (1985) *Studying School Effectiveness.* London: Falmer.

Rutter, M., Maughan, B., Mortimore, P. and Ouston, J. (1979) *Fifteen Thousand Hours.* London: Open Books.

Sands, M. and Kerry, T. (eds) (1982) *Mixed Ability Teaching.* London: Croom Helm.

Schools Council (1980) *Information Skills in the Secondary Curriculum.* Curriculum Bulletin 9. London: Schools Council.

Secretary of State for Education (1990) *Letter to Chief Education Officers*, 10 December.

Sharp, C. (1995) *School Entry and the Impact of Season of Birth on Attainment.* Slough: National Foundation for Educational Research.

Skinner, B.F. (1968) *The Technology of Teaching.* New York: Appleton Century Crofts.

Sotto, E. (1994) *When Teaching Becomes Learning: a Theory and Practice of Teaching.* London: Cassell Education.

Sumner, R. (1987) *The Role of Testing in Schools.* Windsor: NFER-Nelson.

Surrey County Council (1994) *Teacher and Headteacher Appraisal: the Surrey Scheme.* Kingston: Surrey County Council.

Sutton, C. (ed.) (1981) *Communication in the Classroom.* London: Hodder and Stoughton.

Teacher Training Agency (1994) *Profile of Teacher Competences Consultation on Draft Guidance.* Letter from the Chairman. London: TTA.

Tizard, B., Blatchford, P., Burke, J., Farquhar, C. and Lewis, I. (1988) *Young Children at School in the Inner City.* Brighton: Lawrence Erlbaum Associates.

Tomlinson, P. (1995) *Understanding Mentoring: Reflective Strategies for School-based Teacher Preparation.* Buckingham: Open University Press.

Vygotsky, L.S. (1978) *Mind in Society: the Development of Higher Psychological Processes.* Cambridge, MA: Harvard University Press.

Waterhouse, P. (1983) *Managing the Learning Process.* Maidenhead: McGraw-Hill.

Wheldall, K. and Merrett, F. (1984) *Positive Teaching: the Behavioural Approach.* London: Unwin Educational Books.

Wilce, H. (1985) A chance to be equal, *Times Educational Supplement,* 9 September 19.

Wood, D. and Wood, H. (1988) Questioning versus student initiative, in J.T. Dillon (ed.) *Question and Discussion: a Multidisciplinary Study.* Norwood, NJ: Ablex.

Woods, P. (1989) Stress and the teacher's role, in M. Cole and S. Walker (eds) *Teaching and Stress.* Milton Keynes: Open University Press.

Wragg, E.C. (1984) *Classroom Teaching Skills.* London: Croom Helm/Routledge.

Wragg, E.C. and Brown, G. (1993) *Explaining.* London: Routledge.

INDEX

ENCOURAGING LEARNING
TOWARDS A THEORY OF THE LEARNING SCHOOL

Jon Nixon, Jane Martin, Penny McKeown and Stewart Ranson

This book offers a radical critique of both the Government's agenda for educational reform and of the various alternative agendas that have been proposed in recent years. It is based upon original research by a distinguished inter-disciplinary author team.

The focus of the book is on the work of secondary schools located in contexts of disadvantage and on the overwhelming need to motivate young people and to foster in them a sense of purpose and optimism for the future.

In particular, the authors discuss:

- how broader social trends impact upon schools as they move towards the year 2000;
- ways of understanding the low educational expectations of many young people and their disaffected attitude towards schooling;
- strategies by which schools can motivate students to take responsibility for their own learning;
- ways of working in partnership with parents and in collaboration with other schools.

The book is based on the premise that if schools in contexts of disadvantage can be made to work, then schools in other more favourable contexts will have much to learn from them. The book will be of interest to teachers and headteachers, educational policy makers and social scientists with a professional interest in educational and management issues.

Contents
Preface – The limits of the present reform agendas – Towards a theory of learning – The learning school I – The learning school II – Towards the twenty-first century – References – Index.

160pp   0 335 19087 1 (Paperback)   0 335 19088 X (Hardback)

RACISM AND ANTIRACISM IN REAL SCHOOLS

David Gillborn

- How are 'race' and racism implicated in education policy and practice?
- What does effective antiracism look like in practice?
- How can teachers and school students be encouraged to think critically about their racialized assumptions and actions?

In exploring these questions David Gillborn makes a vital contribution to the debate on 'race' and racism in education. He focuses on racism in the policy, research, theory and practice of education, and includes the first major study of antiracism at the level of whole-school management and classroom practice. The voices of teachers and school students bring the issues to life, and illustrate the daily problems of life in urban schools. This is a fascinating picture of the key matters facing managers, classroom teachers and their students as schools struggle to develop strong and workable approaches to anti-racist education. It is accompanied by a critical review of current debates and controversies concerning 'race', ethnicity and identity.

Arguing for a critical return to the concept of 'race', *Racism and Antiracism in Real Schools* represents an important addition to the literature on the theory and practice of education in a racist society.

Contents
Racism and schooling – Part I: 'Race', research and policy – Discourse and policy – Racism and research – Theorizing identity and antiracism - Part II: 'Race' and educational practice – The politics of school change – Antiracism and the whole school – Antiracism in the classroom – Student perspectives – Rethinking racism and antiracism – Notes – References – Name index – Subject index.

240pp   0 335 19092 8 (Paperback)   0 335 19093 6 (Hardback)

TEACHERS TALK ABOUT TEACHING
COPING WITH CHANGE IN TURBULENT TIMES

Judith Bell (ed.)

This book considers the impact of some of the far-reaching educational reforms intro-duced in the UK during the last decade, from the point of view of those people who have been required to implement them. All the contributors are, or were, teachers and all are committed to providing the best possible education for school students. Their views on the impact of some of the reforms provide an insight into what it is like to work in schools today and the effect the many demands placed on them have had on their lives. They consider the impact of the National Curriculum (and the associated methods of assessment), career prospects, appraisal, the changed role of governors, the influence of Local Management of Schools and the low morale of many teachers. Throughout the book, the unifying threads are how teachers are coping with change and ways in which their interpretation of autonomy and professionalism differ from those of some ministers and administrators. These messages from the 'coalface' are worthy of serious consideration by all who have a concern for quality education and for the well-being of learners and teachers alike.

Contents

Introduction – PART 1: Changing teaching: Teachers coping with change – Teachers out of control – Teachers autonomy under siege? – PART 2: Careering teachers: New to teaching – In mid-career – From middle to senior management – Leaving the profession – Revisiting classrooms – PART 3: Moving to local management: Not all plain sailing – Governors and teachers: the costs of LMS – PART 4: Subject to change: Careers education: the fight for recognition – At the Core: 'Oh to be in England!' – Postscript – References – Index.

Contributors
Judith Bell, Ken Bryan, Rosemary Chapman, Karen Cowley, Ann Hanson, Jill Horder, Gill Richardson, John Ross, Andrew Spencer, Peter Swientozielskyj, Lorna Unwin, Stephen Waters.

144pp   0 335 19174 6 (Paperback)